The Elusive Elephant: Mama's African Adventure

An action-packed true story of perseverance in the wilds of Africa

Memoir of

Jean Roberts Hodges

The Elusive Elephant: Mama's African Adventure

This Book is Dedicated to:

The many selfless workers who care for and rehabilitate animals who have been harmed or orphaned due to inhumane practices such as poaching.

Acknowledgements:

Thanks to my family and friends who have supported and helped me with my book. Special appreciation to: Kathy Richardson, Bob Booth, Bailee Christensen Skog, Judy Goad, Shannon Brown, Justin & Leilani Zufelt.

Preface

In 1896, far-sighted animal protectionists began carving out the now famous Selous Game Reserve in Tanzania, Africa. This has saved the country's vulnerable wildlife from harm and possible extinction. The massive reserve is twice the size of the state of Maryland and is the largest untouched body of wilderness left on the African Continent. The Selous has had little human disturbance since no permanent habitation and no unauthorized outsiders, like tourists, are allowed. Game managers monitor their animals 24/7 and scientifically issue quotas per species. Controlling the game numbers is essential since the Selous must provide the resources necessary to maintain the health and wellbeing of its growing population.

The reserve has not only succeeded in keeping a balance of nature, but also generates sufficient funds to help protect its iconic wildlife from danger, especially poaching. Here Earth's most magnificent creatures flourish while roaming freely in their natural habitat. In 1982, due to the Selous' globally significant population of elephants and its wide variety of wildlife habitats, the reserve received international protection from UNESCO as a World Heritage Site.

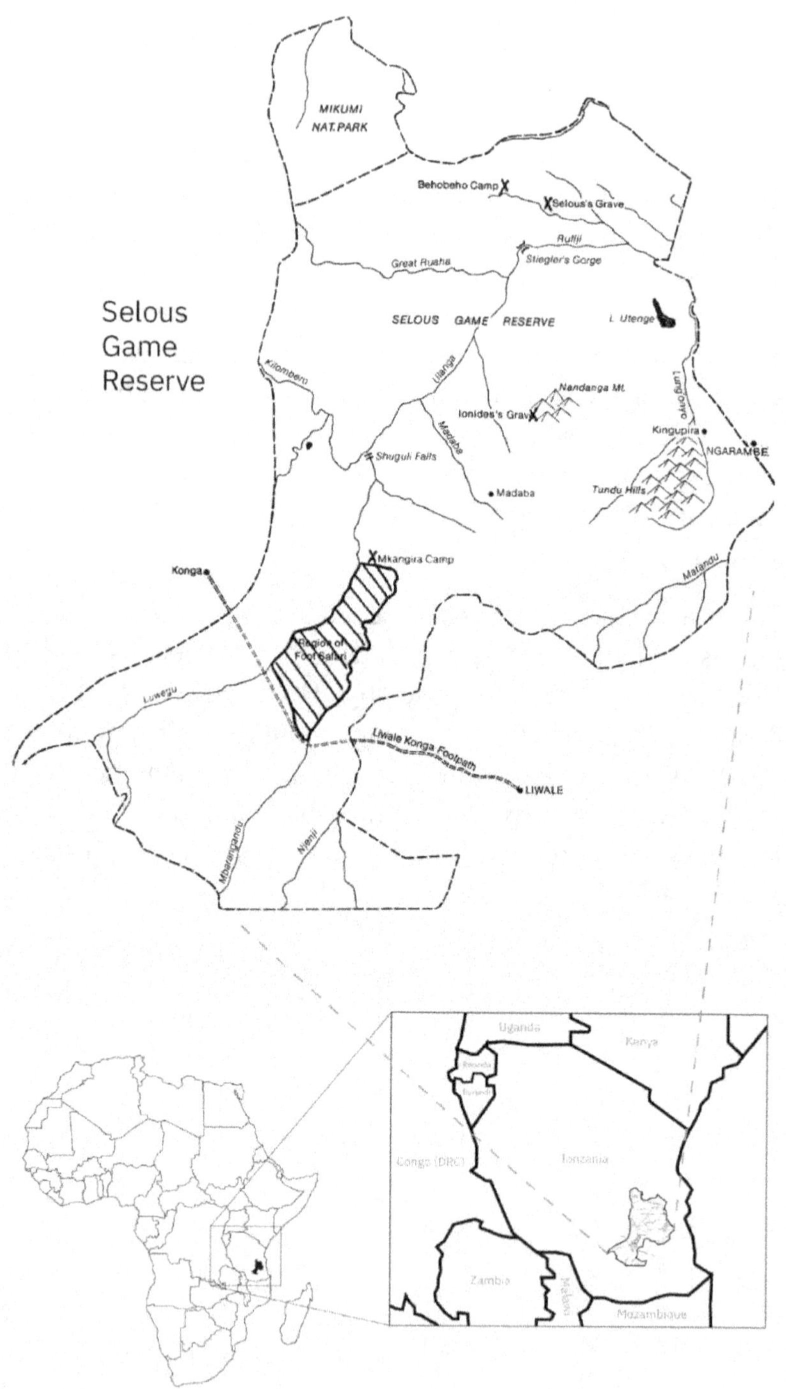

Selous
Game
Reserve
MIKUMI NAT. PARK
Behobeho Camp
Selous's Grave
Ruffji
Great Ruaha
Stiegler's Gorge
SELOUS GAME RESERVE
L. Utenge
Kilombero
Nandanga Mt.
Ionides's Grave
Kingupira
Lung'onyo
NGARAMBE
Shuguli Falls
Madaba
Tundu Hills
Mkangira Camp
Konga
Region of Foot Safari
Matandu
Luwegu
Liwale Konga Footpath
LIWALE
Mbarangandu
Njenji
Uganda
Kenya
Rwanda
Burundi
Congo (DRC)
Tanzania
Zambia
Mozambique

Introduction

My husband, an expert archer, agreed to participate in an experimental project, in East Africa, with the Tanzanian Game Conservation Department. The success of his expedition would be crucial in determining if future bow safaris could be an additional source of revenue for their Selous Game Reserve.

To support my husband's endeavor, I reluctantly left my secure home environment and five children, in Idaho, to make a daily written record of his daring bow adventure in Tanzania.

It was mid-September 1986 when we finally arrived in the Selous Reserve after a year of intense preparation! When the wheels of our charter plane touched down on the desolate dirt landing strip I experienced feelings ranging from exhilaration to fear.

Once our safari personnel arrived, we began the long journey toward the main campsite. While traveling in our jeep caravan, I drank deeply from the astonishing natural wonders that greeted me, an unlikely novice, eager to explore this rarely seen animal refuge. If I had ever wondered what Earth looked like, in the Garden of Eden, then this untouched paradise gave me a clue. I marveled at things like anthills taller than our tent, and miles of bush country full of exotic animals and strange thorn riddled vegetation. The thrill of being in a haven, dedicated to wildlife preservation, touched my soul, and produced within me an African rhythm that I danced to for 21 days.

A world-renowned guide, with years of experience in dealing with wild animals, led our bow expedition. In addition to supervising his safari personnel, he kept us and our documentary film crew safe. We were an interesting mix of male, female, Black, white, and of differing ages and varying degrees of education.

Soon after arriving, we left the safety of the main base and moved miles away to a remote unsecure area. A tent encampment erected under a large mango tree, became our home for 19 days.

Trying to keep up with my adventurous male companions put me, the only women on safari, in many life-threatening situations. These adrenalin-charged events made an indelible impression on my mind that I will never forget.

Taking a mental stroll back to my Selous experiences invariably sparks thoughts of the ruthless grassfires we endured. The many times we threw caution to the wind congers up memories of sleepless nights spent in the tree blind with hungry lions just 15 feet below.

Africa is also the genesis of my darkest fears such as when armed authorities detained us, when lions came into camp, when a scorpion stung me, and when an elephant charged!

Our expedition proved to be as tough as the animals we were seeking. After three long weeks, this adventurous undertaking had taxed all of us to our emotional and physical limits, and almost to death...

Table of Contents

BONUS:
Center Section contains 10 pages of original photographs.

Chapter 1

Leaving at Last

I was already awake when my alarm broke the early morning silence. It was September 15, 1986, in Hibbard, a small farming community in Eastern Idaho. As I rolled out of bed, the feeling of fall was evident in the early morning air. I quickly dressed in the comfortable clothing I had laid out for the long journey. I grabbed my carryon bag and tiptoed down the hall to look at my 5 sleeping children, all snuggled up in their comforters. Leaving them for an extended period was not something I was comfortable with-or happy about doing. I had made every effort to ensure that they would be properly cared for during our absence. Our nanny and her husband lived on the premises and a backup assistant would also be there to help. Anxiety for my children's well-being was tugging at my heart strings to the point that I had to leave before I became completely unglued. I descended the stairs and checked once again to make sure the power of attorney paperwork was still on the fireplace mantle. Our friends, the Paige's, would be several children richer in case we did not return.

It was still dark as I stepped out onto the front steps. A teenage neighbor boy, Jerry Munn, was helping my husband Will, finish loading his paraphernalia into his dual-cabbed truck. Jerry ran to grab my bag and placed it in the back seat. We all agreed that it would be best if I drove because Will had stayed up all night assembling his gear. We thanked Jerry, hopped into the truck, and turned the engine on to get the heater going. As we fastened our safety belts,

Will turned towards me and with a smirk on his tired but excited face said, "Still want to go?"

"Why not? Someone has to make sure your remains get back home," I responded in jest.

Chapter 1

As dawn broke, we rounded the end of our long gravel driveway, turned left, and drove past the familiar terrain on the outskirts of Rexburg.

I wondered what the landscape would look like where we were headed.

Pretty much everyone in our small community knew about our long-awaited trip. Family and friends had wished us well, but I am sure they questioned our sanity when they found out that Will intended to tackle dangerous animals in such an unconventional manner.

We sped south, along a nearly empty highway, toward Utah. I knew little about what was ahead of me and hoped to pick my husband's brain about our upcoming journey to the other side of the world. Unfortunately, he opted to go over his to-do list for the 'umpteenth' time. I was used to his endless preoccupation with what I secretly called his 'magnificent obsession.'

In the silence, time and distance slipped smoothly past the hood of our vehicle. My thoughts drifted back to an evening months earlier. As I recall, I was putting away the last of the dinner dishes when my usually calm and collected husband came bursting into the kitchen.

"Guess what?" he blurted out, visibly bursting with excitement. I joked, "You won the lottery."

"No, this is much better than that."

Wow, then this must really be something good.

"We've been given permission from the Tanzanian Government to help their conservation experts, in the Selous Game Reserve, with an ever-present balance of nature problem."

"Who's we?"

"You and me. You don't think I'm going back to Africa without you?" he said while giving me a big hug. "Besides, I need your writing talents to capture this historic experiment."

Managing a faint smile, I queried, "What makes it so historic?"

"Well, let me explain. Over the years, Tanzanian game experts have successfully managed the wild animal population in their reserve. But with that success comes an ever-increasing number of animals. This situation constantly puts pressure on the Selous to supply the food necessary to properly feed its inhabitants. A food shortage adversely affects the balance of nature needed to feed its thousands of animals, not to mention 110,000 hungry elephants.

Game managers scientifically developed a successful plan that benefits both man and beast. The money raised from issuing short-term hunting permits keeps the herd numbers in check and produces the funds necessary to support and protect the animals year-round from illegal hunting practices like poaching. Those who receive permits must also pay for game personnel to accompany them night and day to make sure the reserve's strict rules are adhered to."

Before I could say anything, Will added, "My permit to cull certain animals is totally unique. I will not be using the customary high-powered rifle. Guess how I'm allowed to take my animals?"

"You don't mean big game, like elephants, using your compound bow?" I was secretly hoping he would say, NO.

With both hands held high in the air he shouted, "Yeah, that's the best part; my permit includes taking designated male animals including a bull elephant!"

I blurted out, "You've got to be kidding. Has that ever been done?"

"Yes, world records show that one or two other archers have succeeded in taking an African bull elephant with a non-poisonous arrow."

Will hoped that, if successful, his attempt might open doors to allow more bow hunting in Africa. Doors presently closed by skeptical safari companies, game guides, and government bureaucrats.

I slowly lowered myself onto a bar stool at the kitchen counter attempting to get my head around his BIG pronouncement. I could not decide whether to laugh or cry.

I knew I should be supportive but, to me tackling dangerous animals using a sharp, pointed stick decorated with colorful feathers seemed as absurd, as young David's offer to slay the giant Goliath with a slingshot.

Will continued, "The Tanzania bow experiment may prove to be a good alternative to culling animals using rifles, fitted with long-range scopes, which can take down animals relatively easy. By using a bow, the animals have a decided advantage. They are on their own familiar turf. I must track them on foot, then maneuver myself close enough to get a shot off. All this is so time-consuming that it is simply impossible for bow hunters to kill large numbers of game. In fact, the animal's odds are much greater than mine."

To keep peace in the family, I decided to appear open-minded on the subject.

As the months rolled by, I continued having questions, fears, and concerns; but I was finally able to grasp the plight of the animals living in the Selous. The reserve was only so big, and their best chance of survival was staying within its boundaries. With so many mouths to feed, some older males had to go for everyone's sake. Their sanctuary, although vast, was surrounded by a human population. Wild animals, foraging for food 'off campus,' are a dangerous nuisance to the poor natives, so they naturally kill their intruders to protect and feed their families.

I fully expected that something or someone would prevent me from making the journey, but over the next year I dutifully prepared just to be on the safe side. After all, I was no stranger to disappointment. Back in 1983, I was all excited about the prospects of accompanying Will to Africa. My plans were dramatically altered when I became pregnant, and my doctor wisely advised against making the long, hard journey.

Will had the advantage over me as to what to expect in the African bush. However, being in ta reserve would differ in many aspects. The South African trip was on a private game ranch and was considerably less dangerous than this Tanzanian project would be. These animals would be wary, fearless, and unpredictable, particularly since Will was only equipped with bow and arrow.

Walking briskly for 6 miles a day was the minimum recommended exercise to be able to keep pace with the men. I joined some friends on their walks which helped keep me motivated. While exercising, I conjured up romantic notions about what Africa would be like. During the day, I would observe a variety of fascinating animals in their natural habitat. At night, while sitting around the campfire, we would discuss the day's exciting events. Being a novice, I entertained the ridiculous notion of bringing along a bag of marshmallows to toast. I later decided against it, figuring that they would be mashed to smithereens by the time we arrived.

My friends were excited for me. They told me not to worry about the kids. "Go and support your husband but, most importantly, enjoy yourself. It is the ultimate Mom's Getaway! We'll worry for you and make sure the kids are well taken care of while you're gone."

In the ensuing months, I became more open to becoming a part of this endeavor usually reserved only for 'macho' males. Admittedly, this trip would be a wonderful opportunity for Will and me to share an unforgettable experience together.

My mind was brought into the present as we drove into Salt Lake City. We met up with our documentary film makers. Brian Sullivan would be our director/cameraman, and Dennis Shirley, the audio technician. Brian came highly recommended by T. C. Christensen, a successful film maker. Brian held a master's degree in motion picture history with emphasis on film direction and cinematography.

It was our good fortune that he could fit the long trip into his schedule. Brian had worked on numerous feature-length movies, educational films, documentaries, and television projects. He was an annually invited participant at Robert Redford's Sundance Institute, where in 1984, he served as Director of Photography.

Dennis brought other expertise to the team. He was a seasoned Wildlife Manager for the State of Utah. This rugged outdoorsman was also an avid archer and had accompanied Will on previous hunts. Both men assured Will that all the 'bugs' had been worked out of the new filming equipment that Will had purchased specifically for this project. Like me, it was their first trip to Africa, and filming there was an opportunity they were anxious to be a part of.

The men sorted the gear into seven heavy-duty blue river bags, while I ran around town picking up all the last-minute items that we needed. Will and I took three of the bags with us and left the remaining four for the Utahns to bring. We were scheduled to leave a few days ahead of the camera crew. Will had been advised that we would probably never be able to get through all the Tanzanian Government's 'red tape' to make this film. We were admonished to be very low-key and proceed on our own with the project. To further ensure our successful entry into Tanzania, we booked two different airlines on different days. If government officials saw too much professional camera equipment entering their country, rumor had it that they would either confiscate it or refuse us entry.

We gathered our things and headed for the U.S. Customs office to declare our belongings and complete the necessary paperwork for entering Tanzania. As we left our camera crew, the men excitedly slapped each other on the back saying, "The next time we see you, we'll be in Africa!"

The sceptic within each of us was sure there was no place left on earth this remote and full of untamed wildlife, but the adventurer in us hoped it was true.

Will and I checked into a hotel before our flight the following day. My husband still did not get much rest, as he continued checking every detail before leaving. He explained, "Whatever we need must be taken by us, because there is no place to buy it in a Third World country."

We arrived the next morning at the Salt Lake airport. While we were waiting to depart, I wandered into the nearest news stand to buy something to read on my long trip. Several of the news magazine's cover stories featured a 16-hour ordeal that had happened a few days earlier. Arabs had hijacked a Pan American jumbo jet at the Karachi Airport that ended in a bloodbath. I had been so busy with my preparations that I was oblivious to world events. The string of airplane hijacks, occurring on an all too frequent basis, made me feel extremely vulnerable.

This fear caused me to visually scrutinize passengers onboard our flight to Chicago for any telltale signs that they might be terrorist's intent on carrying out another evil plot. We had not left the ground, set foot in Africa, or seen a wild animal, yet the dangerous uncertainties of world travel unnerved me. I began feeling the trepidation of leaving my peaceful community and entering an unfamiliar world fraught with danger.

Reminiscent Journey

Will turned to me as our plane was about to take off. "It's hard to believe that after all our hard work we're finally on our way." I wholeheartedly agreed that indeed it was great to be on our way to Africa. The powerful jet engines thrust us heavenward, and we disappeared into the billowy clouds over the Salt Lake valley. Before long Will was fast asleep. The man has a gift. He calls sleep, and it comes no matter what, no matter where. Rays of sunlight were streaming through the window onto him, bringing out the red highlights in his graying brown hair. He slept most of the trip since he had only gotten three hours of sleep in the past 72 hours.

I settled back and read my magazine, which was full of pictures and details about how the perpetrators had executed their hijacking operation. Once I had read my fill of the tragic story, I used my quiet time to write about the myriads of preparations we had made over the last year.

There is a metaphor that says, 'Rome was not built in a day,' which was the case with our project. Africa had indeed become a heavy taskmaster, demanding our time, money, and energy, long before we ever set foot on her soil.

Once Will was given permission from the Tanzania's Game Conservation Department to do an experimental bow hunt. He hired Burt Klineberger's worldwide referral service to locate safari guides and outfitters that operated in Tanzania. Gerald Pasanisi, owner of Tanganyika Wildlife Safaris agreed to handle our bow adventure.

Francois, an experienced hunting guide, came highly recommended as the man with the bush savvy and courage needed to lead such a risky expedition. Everyone agreed that Francois deserved his stellar reputation as one of Africa's foremost white hunters. Will succeeded in booking him at the optimal time of the year for bow hunting.

Once the safari details were finalized, Will turned his attention to researching the animals he would most likely encounter. He studied their anatomy so he would know where to aim to make a swift, humane kill. His most daunting task was developing arrows and broadheads, a large cutting point assembly attached to an arrow's shaft. He experimented with various ideas and talked with numerous archers, equipment dealers, and manufacturers before inventing a stronger aluminum shaft. His experiments included filling the shaft with sand, lead plugs, and even fitting one shaft inside another. These proved futile because they were not aerodynamically accurate. The shaft that finally proved successful was the one he filled with water. This design had the strength needed to penetrate the toughened hides of African animals.

Leaving no stone unturned, Will flew to Seattle, Washington to better his archery skills. He spent time training with Bob Markworth, a world-famous trick shot artist.

Will, now 53-years-old, knew he must get into top physical condition to withstand the rigors of this extremely tough expedition. He shed 30 pounds from his six-foot one-inch frame and exercised religiously. He trimmed, firmed, and strengthened his upper torso for the power needed to pull his 90 to 100-pound compound bows. I had no clue that he must pull the entire weight of the bow using only three fingers. First, middle, and ring finger.

For months prior to the hunt, the obsessed archer practiced at least once a day. He positioned archery targets at varying distances and heights around our property. On several occasions, he suffered serious muscle strains. Taking time for his body to heal was frustrating as it cost him precious practice time.

Our upcoming adventure created an air of excitement, which spread amongst the many hunting enthusiasts in the surrounding area. Will became a sort of homegrown celebrity. For months, our home was a gathering place where curious, supportive men, of all ages, came to take part in the never-ending preparations. Will attributed much of the credit for his being able to reach his goal, to a couple of his bow hunting enthusiast, Dondavid Powell and Dana Green. They got themselves roped into pulling the powerful bows during many lengthy sessions, while testing various shafts using different broad heads. A chronograph helped them determine the speed in feet per second as the arrow left the bow. Cement cinder block targets were used to replicate an animal's thick hide.

Since this excursion would be reminiscent of an old-fashioned classic safari, Will determined that it should be filmed as a documentary. He read many books on the subject and spent untold hours on the phone talking with film and wildlife experts. After extensive research and trips to Hollywood, he purchased the Artifex 16mm camera. This equipment could take quality footage and hold up under the punishment it would receive in the bush.

Next came locating a suitable film crew. He interviewed numerous candidates. They must be experienced in filming animals in the wild, plus have physical stamina and fortitude to shoot footage under trying conditions for three long weeks.

In addition, Will also bought our crew's camouflage clothing, canteens, river bags, medications, spare parts, insect repellant, backpacks, etc. On top of that, he obtained airline and hotel reservations, visas, and passports, and made sure we all received a LONG list of immunizations. After months of preparation, we were finally ready to go.

The pressure in my ears indicated that our flight was about to land in Chicago. We were pleasantly surprised when our seating arrangements to Amsterdam were considerably better than expected. Our stewardess said that because our fight was overbooked, we had been upgraded to the more comfortable business class.

As we taxied out onto the runway, Will excitedly said, "Wow, look at that. The whole top of that plane has been blown off." I quickly peered out his window and got a glimpse of the damaged airliner. It was downright chilling to see the devastation caused by those wanting worldwide attention drawn to their radical causes.

The wheels had barely lifted off when I got my first taste of international travel. Will, in his usual friendly manner, struck up a conversation with an interesting couple seated across the aisle. They were living in Kenya on a working mission for the Mennonite Church. The man turned out to be, none other than, a camel salesman who was attempting to introduce this desert beast of burden to the reluctant Africans. He excitedly extolled the advantages of the camel over the domestic livestock presently used by the tribes. We laughed when he told us that the place where he buys his camels is appropriately called 'Camelot.'

There certainly were no camel salesmen in Idaho.

During the night, as if on the wings of a bird, we glided beyond the portals of familiar surroundings into an unknown world. Far beneath lay the waters of the Atlantic Ocean. Will managed to grab some additional rest between the dinner and breakfast meal service on our Flying Dutchman aircraft. I, on the other hand, am not able to sleep sitting upright, so I spent a good portion of the night trying various futile attempts to doze off. We flew inland and emerged, along with a new day, over Holland as the sun arose over its capital city. This was my first trip to the European continent, and I found the various travelers milling around in Schiphol Airport quite fascinating.

After boarding our DC-10 destined for Tanzania, the full impact of our long-awaited undertaking suddenly hit me. I turned to Will and excitedly exclaimed, "Pinch me quick to make sure I'm not dreaming. I'm headed INTO AFRICA!"

I began contemplating the reasons why I had come on this trip. Because I have always been the curious type, because of the amazing variety of wildlife, because of my opportunity to be part of what most people only dream of doing, and because I want to be an eyewitness to my husband's successes.

Our itinerary showed a non-stop flight to Tanzania's capital city. Shortly after takeoff the purser announced, "The flight to Khartoum will be 5 hour and 45 minutes." So, this was NOT a flight to Dar-es-Salaam. It seems that on certain days of the week, this flight makes an intermediary stop in the Sudan, and today was one of those times. I fumbled around in the seat pocket to find a map showing exactly where the Sudan was located. I found it all right, and I was not overjoyed at the prospect of landing so close to the Middle East, in a country not on the friendliest terms with our government. The bomb-riddled jet, at Chicago's O'Hare Field, flooded back into my mind. We had gone to great lengths to keep from putting ourselves in harm's way. Now we were captive passengers heading for the capital city of Khartoum. There was nothing we could do about it.

It has been said that 'variety is the spice of life.' The passengers on this flight were a highly seasoned melting pot full of many races and cultures. There were Black women dressed in colorful fabrics, mysterious looking bearded men in long flowing white robes, nuns, safari hunters, businessmen, families, turban topped travelers, and women in flowing floor-length dresses with colorful dots on their foreheads. A noisy bunch of Italians were seated across the aisle. All night long, they enthusiastically chattered amongst themselves using sweeping hand gestures to emphasize their points of view. Their incessant conversations did not disturb Will but made it impossible for me to sleep.

We landed in Khartoum without incident, but we were not allowed to disembark during the one hour refueling stop. Off in the distance a fellow passenger pointed out a Russian airliner boarding passenger for Moscow. It was the first time I had ever seen one of their aircraft. I felt uncomfortable being in a place openly courting a Communist country.

A friendly male passenger suggested that once we were airborne, we should catch a glimpse of the confluence of the Blue and White Nile Rivers. Sure enough, we flew right over the spectacular wide, shimmering waters beneath, which were quite a contrast to the arid terrain around Khartoum. The pilot's intercom message informed us that a recent desert sandstorm had cast a haze over the entire region. This caused the unattractive desert landscape to appear even more uninviting.

The final leg of our three-and-a-half-hour journey to our final destination went smoothly, but I was feeling restless and irritable after being cooped up in a plane for days, to say nothing of the sleep deprivation, and nine-hour time difference. To put it mildly, I was looking forward to getting down to Earth.

Our stewardess handed us a certificate indicating our aircraft had just crossed the Equator. Will leaned my direction to give me a piece of welcome news, "The Equator delineates the northernmost boundary of Tanzania, so we'll be landing shortly."

Discovering Dar-es-Salaam

We were relieved to see that all our belongings had arrived in Tanzania. We received a warm, friendly greeting to the capital city, Dar-es-Salaam, from Dick, an employee of our safari company. He was also busy assisting three other groups from our flight. We noticed that if Dick had not been on a first name basis with the customs personnel, we might still be stuck in the slow-moving lines. One of his hunting parties was experiencing some sort of paperwork difficulties. We watched in disbelief as the authorities confiscated their hunting rifles. Dick confidently promised his distraught clientele, "Don't worry, I'll get them back tomorrow."

The massive mounds of baggage from Dick's safari clients busied 18 eager porters. They sorted and hauled everyone's belongings into vehicles, which would deliver us to our respective destinations. The sun was low in the sky as we left Dar's city limits. The 25-mile trip to our hotel opened our eyes to Third World realities. This country did not look anything like the attractive photographs I had just perused in the flight magazine. If fact, Tanzania turned out to be one of the world's poorest countries.

The trip to our hotel took almost an hour due to our drivers constant need to dodge numerous potholes in their deteriorating roads. Once the sun was down, it became evident there were few residents who had the benefit of electricity. Thus, the locals were drawn to the few places where lights and loud music provided them with a place of refuge from their dark dwellings.

As our hotel came into view, the quaint quintessential atmosphere that one expects to find in Africa appeared. The Bahari Beach Hotel's beautifully landscaped property with clusters of traditional thatched roofed bungalows. Each round dwelling, fashioned of ruff-hewn, native stone, housed four guestrooms: two upper and two lower. Luckily, we were assigned to an upstairs room with a balcony. After the porter left, we went out to enjoy a view of the shimmering moonlit waters of the Indian Ocean.

We unpacked a few essentials, then fell into bed about 1 a.m. After being confined in an airplane seat for so long, it felt heavenly to lie down and stretch out. The rhythmic waves slapping gently against the shoreline below soon lulled us into a most welcomed slumber.

I would have been content to remain curled up in the crisp, white sheets, but Will rousted me out, anxious 'to get the show on the road.' Being half asleep, I was not paying close attention to what I was supposed to be doing. Out of habit, I began brushing my teeth using the tap water instead of the potable water provided by the hotel. Suddenly, I became wide awake remembering how impure the water had been. It was so bad that when I had filled the sink, to wash my face, I saw all sorts of unidentifiable 'floaties' in the swirling liquid. I prepared for the worst and threw some dysentery preventatives into my bag.

Will and I descended the steps and leisurely strolled toward the hotel's restaurant in the warm sunshine. The hibiscus, bougainvillea, and fragrant plumeria were in full bloom as we passed beneath tall palm trees swaying in the pleasant ocean breezes. This tropical paradise had a ring of familiarity to it since Hawaii and Costa Rica were places, we had once lived. From a distance, the hotel appeared well-kempt, but as we neared the pool area, we noticed signs of wear and neglect on beach chairs, and the paint was peeling off the pool in numerous places.

Inside the ocean-side restaurant, we were seated by an affable English-speaking waiter wearing a starched white jacket. We explained that we were expecting Dick to join us. While waiting, Will and I enjoyed a rare opportunity to just sit and visit uninterrupted by the usual family and business matters. We became fascinated by the birds soaring gracefully overhead that periodically swooped down into the shallows attempting to catch their breakfast. While we waited for Dick, the waiter surprised us with a tasty variety of tree-ripened local produce: bananas, papayas, guava, passion fruit, pineapple and, my favorite, mango.

Dick never came so following our breakfast, we went to his room to see why he had not shown up. After several loud knocks on his door, our bare-chested, sleepy-eyed friend opened the door wearing a long colorful piece of fabric knotted at the waist. He sheepishly apologized for having overslept, then quickly dressed and came to our room. The men finalized arrangements for Dick to help our camera crew through customs at 6 a.m. the following morning. He also agreed to book us an afternoon flight down to the game reserve.

"Would you like to go sightseeing this afternoon?" Dick queried. "It'll be your only chance." When we showed interest, he promised, "I'll send a driver to show you around this afternoon." Once Dick left, Will assembled his archery equipment for a target shooting session down on the beach. "Jean, after your swim, you'd better get some local money for our shopping spree."

I went to the hotel cashier and asked to change $500 worth of traveler's checks into Tanzanian shillings. The attractive Black women, seated officiously inside her cashier's cage, affirmed that it would be possible. The cashier watched me scrawl Jean Roberts across each check, gathered up the checks, glanced my way, then made a phone call. The strange way she acted made me feel uneasy. Many thoughts raced through my mind. *This was a large sum of money. Were they planning to rob me? What was that 'call' all about?*

After speaking to someone in Swahili for several minutes, she ended her conversation and explained, "Madam, I can only cash $50 worth right now." She suggested that I return, in a few hours, for the remainder of the money. I agreed but was still feeling unsure about the situation. I was relieved once I had gotten the large amount of money and was safely back inside my room.

At 2 p.m., our driver and his male companion met us in the main lobby to chauffeur us around the area. Our English-speaking driver explained, "Our inhabitants speak Swahili; a term meaning coastal people. Historians believe Arab traders began settling East African coastal villages about the time of Christ. The native and Arab cultures mixed and developed into the Swahili civilization."

Dick had arranged for us to visit a must see 'tourist trap.' However, the highly touted ivory market turned out to be nothing more than a few open-air rusty, metal stalls, with men seated on the ground carving various African figures. We were not impressed with the costliness of and the poor workmanship of their wares. Will asked the driver to take us to the city center in hopes that the shopping there would be better. This, however, was not the case. There was little to buy and what was for sale was of poor quality and of no interest to us.

As we drove in and around the city, I made several observations. The economic situation here was visibly desperate. The stores had little or nothing to sell. The despair amongst its population was present everywhere. The driver indicated that this country's sad situation emanated from a plethora of causes. "Over the years, multiple sultans, Germans, and Brits have ruled us. Once the Germans were defeated in World War II, German East Africa became a British trust until we gained our independence in 1961. Once independent from Britain, one of our locals became Prime Minster and tried another failed attempt at socialism. At that point, the citizens realized that when we threw the whites out, we ended up 'throwing the baby out with the bath water.' As the last gasps of Colonialism faded, so did our economy. Our people have endured scandals, violence, and lack of funds. This coupled with insufficient knowledge has caused our country to descend into our present state-of-affairs. Now reduced to a 'faded rose,' we long for a breath of capitalism to once again blow our way."

The terrain around Dar was flat and most of its citizens walked. Their well-worn earthen footpaths were strewn with litter, and an amazing assortment of makeshift stands had been erected to service the needs of the weary walking masses. Those that could afford it rode in overcrowded buses or caught rides on anything that moved. I only saw a few bicycles and even fewer motorcycles. There were trucks and some cars, but they were almost always driven by whites. The natives simply could not afford transportation or the steep petrol prices.

People-watching here was fascinating. We saw East Asian looking women modestly robed in long flowing attire with veiled faces. Muslim males were easily recognizable by their small fabric hats with various intricate patterns woven into them. The more pious men dressed in long white tops with matching trousers. We were told these men have many wives.

I especially enjoyed the traditionally attired African women whose bright fabrics were gracefully wrapped around their trim torsos. The younger ones were usually toting small children on their backs cleverly intertwined in their mother's fabric dress. Most women had both hands full of something and many were carrying things atop their heads. This included pots, baskets, stacks of wood, large boxes, cases of Pepsi, stalks of bananas, and sacks of grain. You name it; it was adroitly balanced atop the heads of those poor over-burdened women. If 'necessity is the mother of invention' then, in my opinion, these women would win the prize for ingenuity and endurance. The cases of Pepsi were the only visible sign of American commerce. There were no American restaurant chains purveying their burgers, fried chicken, or pizza. These pricy fast-food establishments would not be a profitable venture in this poor country.

I asked our driver, "Would you stop and let me get out to take pictures of these fascinating people?" He said, "Yes, but you must first get their permission before taking their photographs." The driver explained, "Some are unwilling to be photographed because of old superstitious. They still believe that a person's spirit is being captured in the picture."

After being turned down numerous times, the driver helped me convince a young mother, walking along the roadside, to let me take her picture. The adorable child, strapped on her back, kept peeking its inquisitive curly head around to see the white skinned stranger. The mother was accompanied by another woman carrying a large woven basket atop her head. Both women reluctantly paused as I snapped their picture. Afterwards, I profusely thanked and tipped them for their kindness.

We drove away with me waving goodbye to them from the back window. They acknowledged my wave by smiling back at me. My heart ached for their plight.

I also got some shots of their primitive houses, which were constructed of sticks and mud. We stopped to photograph some Black youth playing soccer on the campus of the country's only university. These young boys had obviously never heard about the superstitions because they nearly trampled each other trying to be included in the picture.

Once we arrived back at our hotel, Will generously paid our driver and his companion for their interesting tour. As they drove away, Will shook his head and quietly said to me,

"I can't believe this place. How does anything ever get accomplished here?"

"We're spoiled," I said. "In the states, stores are stocked with a wide variety of quality goods, but here there is literally nothing to buy. They have so little, and in my opinion, their future looks pretty bleak."

When I first learned we were destined for Tanzania, I knew it was located somewhere on the African continent, but exactly where, I had no clue. I never suspected how underdeveloped this country would be. Certainly not a preferred destination that the average tourist would choose to visit. It was basically just a necessary stop on the safari circuit.

Off to a Bad Start

When Brian and Denny's flight landed at 6 a.m., Dick schmoozed the custom agents sufficiently that our camera crew and all their equipment had no problems entering the country. The men were understandably tired after their lengthy journey. Dick took them to the Pasanisi's beach bungalow near our hotel so they could relax and freshen up. Janine, our safari owner's wife, had coincidentally arrived from France on the same flight as our film experts. Dick had arranged for Will and me to meet the three of them for lunch before flying to the reserve.

After swimming I took a short walk to explore the Indian Ocean conveniently located behind our hotel. My walk along the water's edge did not seem to bother the many hungry birds paddling around in the tepid shallows in search of their morning meal. I was intrigued by a group of men who had pulled their rugged dugout canoes onto the beach. They were native fisherman pulling in their fishing net. There were four men on either side tugging on the huge net which contained what I considered to be a meager catch. As I strolled farther down the beach, I was shocked when I stumbled upon a bevy of bare-breasted bathers. *No wonder Will had been so diligent practicing on the beach!* My attention was then diverted by a young Black man walking along the shoreline selling his wares. He offered me beautifully carved busts of native men and women, but unfortunately, I had no money with me. Sadly, I shook my head indicating I could not buy them.

As scheduled, we met for lunch at the hotel's restaurant. The last time we had dined with Brian and Denny was when they stayed with our family for two days getting footage of our safari preparations. They filmed Will out in our yard practice shooting at makeshift 'clay pigeons' fashioned out of balloons. They also explored our big red barn, which Will had transformed into a workshop, indoor archery range, and an upstairs apartment. In addition, they filmed Will working out at the health club and jogging around the neighborhood. Inside the house, they filmed Will's large office which was filled with trophies and memorabilia from previous hunts. The men also filmed our family's dinner table conversations as we discussed our upcoming African trip. Brian felt these short clips would be good filler material to intersperse throughout the documentary.

Dick had booked us on a 2 p.m. flight to the reserve, but we were prevented from checking out of the hotel because the hotel's sole cashier was at lunch. Will and Dick tried every trick in the book to solve our maddening situation, but the desk manager insisted that we could only settle our account with the cashier. Dick drove to the airport as fast as the pothole ridden roads would allow, attempting to postpone our departure for a few hours until we could check out of the hotel. His efforts were, unfortunately, in vain because the pilot had already left for the reserve with only half of our gear and none of his passengers. Dick was livid and embarrassed about this regrettable blunder, which he swore had never happened during his seven-year tenure with the safari company. Since this was the sole charter air service in Dar, we were out of luck until tomorrow.

To make a long story short, we spent another night at the Bahari Beach Hotel. When Mrs. Pasanisi heard of our plight, she came over to our hotel room to apologize and console us. During her visit, she noticed our family picture. I pointed out each child. "Will's son, Rusty, has gorgeous bright, red hair. He is older and does not live with us. Shannon, my musically talented daughter is a high school honor student. These handsome young boys John, Jared, and Brigham are our adorable sibling group. And finally, there's Leilani who was born in Hawaii. She turns three next month." Janine smiled and said, "Jean, you have a beautiful family, and it looks like you have your hands full." I whole-heartedly agreed and said in gist, "No, safari could come close to my hectic, daily schedule over the last few years. I also the local president of a worldwide women's service organization."

I will be forever grateful to Janine who helped alleviate some of my growing concerns about our safety while in the bush. She assured me that Will had chosen the world's best white hunter. "Francois is an extremely competent, highly respected, hunting legend. No one loves animals more or understands them better. If by chance, you find yourselves in a precarious situation, he never does the wrong thing. And, incidentally, no one shoots more cleanly than this Parisian."

Before she left, Janine invited us to be her guests for a fresh lobster dinner that night in the hotel's restaurant. She was also hosting several other safari clients, fellow Americans, who had just returned from their hunt with Francois. She felt we would enjoy a first-hand report from them about their experiences.

That evening, while enjoying the delicious meal, Will seized the opportunity to get a few of his questions answered. "How much game have you seen? What kind of white hunter is Francois? Where have you seen the most elephant?" Will seemed pleased with their answers. After a welcome break from Will's questions, the hunters warned us, "In case you didn't know, no one is allowed to take even a leaf out of the reserve without permission."

At the conclusion of our meal, a spectacular full moon grabbed Brian's attention, and he excused himself to go get the camera from his room to capture the awe-inspiring sight. On the way back, a voluptuous, good-looking, Black women, whose sole English word was 'prostitute,' surprised him with her persistent propositions. We laughed until our sides ached as big Brian excitedly told everyone about his evasion efforts to dodge this tenacious hooker.

Since arriving in Tanzania, none of us had been successful in getting a telephone call through to our families. To put it mildly, Tanzania's phone service was not up to par by American standards. Janine made us laugh with her analysis of the situation, "Phone service here can be frustrating because a call can be cut off by a bird alighting on the telephone wires." Noting our longing to get a call through to our families, she insightfully added, "I promise I'll contact my husband, Gerald, at our office in Nice and have him call from France to let all your families know you're alive and well." While preparing to leave Janine pulled me aside and said, "Jean, please hand-deliver these things to Francois when you see him." I thanked her for her hospitality and assured her that I would deliver the package to him tomorrow.

Will and I strolled hand in hand toward our room under the alluring African night sky. As we crossed over a small bridge, fashioned out of native stone, several of the local frogs began bellowing in loud baritone croaking noises, expressing their apparent displeasure at our trespassing on THEIR territory. As we neared our newly assigned hotel room, Denny called for us to come over to see something unusual. "Hey, look at our unique greeting committee." He pointed up to several bats hanging upside down in the wooden eaves above the entrance to their room. As we left, we all got a laugh as Will teased Brian, "In the morning, we'll be checking your neck for marks left by bats or amorous women." There was no end to the unusual experiences we were having, and we were not on safari yet.

When we left the hotel earlier in the day, our original room had been assigned to other guests. Our new accommodation was anything but luxurious. Only one of the 50-watt light bulbs inside our room functioned and anything not bolted down was missing. The beds were as hard as a rock; a board covered with a paper thin 'mattress.' In addition, the air conditioner was broken and circulating warm air throughput the room. To keep from suffocating, we opened the sliding glass door hoping for a breeze, however, the screen was missing. Consequently, we had no protection from bats, bugs, and who knows what else.

My husband dozed right off as soon as his head hit the pillow. I kept thinking of the wide-open balcony door and the bats we had just seen. *Hopefully, they were not vampires with us on their radar.* I lay on my uncomfortable 'bed,' in the hot dark room, listening to Will's annoying snoring. While contemplating my unpleasant situation, I consoled myself with the thought that just down the road natives had no electricity and slept on floor mats.

Mosquitoes soon entered and began buzzing above me. Realizing they were intent on drilling my anatomy, I used the thin white sheet as a protective shield against the persistent blood suckers. To help pass the long miserable night, I began fantasizing that I was the inventor of a technique to extract intelligence from terrorists who had highjacked airplanes. I would gain my vital information by bringing the villains into a small dark room and strapping them onto the dreaded board 'BED.' My interrogation began by cranking the room's thermostat up to the 'Hot-as-the-Hinges-of-Hades' setting. Next came the ear-piercing sound of non-stop snoring accompanied by a fleet of mosquitoes. These flying aces were graduates of the prestigious 'Blood Sucker Institute' and had been retrofitted with drill bits dipped in a deadly malaria concoction.

If this torture did not loosen the scoundrel's tongues, I would unleash thirsty vampire bats into the sweltering cubical. They would firmly affix themselves onto the culprit's necks and begin sucking the lifeblood out of them. One or a combination of these techniques never failed to loosen the tongues of the most wanton criminals.

My brilliance was being acknowledged at a prestigious ceremony in Washington, D.C. where I was accepting an award from the Pentagon concerning the effectiveness of my 'truth extracting' practices. During the lavish affair, the stage lights were focused on me. As I bowed and thanked the adoring crowds.

RING..RING..RING!!!!

My alarm suddenly went off, which jarred me back into reality from my fantasy. Thirty minutes later, Dick's men were knocking at our door to collect our bags. There was still no dawn as we hurried over to the hotel cashier located in the huge open air, thatched roofed lobby. Unbelievably, we had yet another run in with the cashier while attempting to leave. She said the paperwork showing our room payment was nowhere to be found. Fortunately, Will had pre-paid our bill attempting to avert a repeat performance of yesterday's fiasco. Will dug around in his overstuffed leather briefcase and handed the cashier his copy of the paid bill. The hotel employee, foiled at not being able to extort another night's stay from us, thrust Will's receipt back at him with the indignant look of a police officer in the deep south issuing a costly traffic ticket to a car with Yankee license plates. Knowing Will as I do, that cashier had no idea how close she came to having her hair styled by his taxidermist, with the 'paid in full' receipt stuffed between her teeth!

The sun was now alive, and the sky was changing colors as we drove ever closer to the airport. Along the way, I mulled over in my mind the encounters we had experienced in this fascinating and equally exasperating country. The culture shock that I experienced in Tanzania caused me to appreciate my country even more deeply.

Will was full of his usual questions concerning the upcoming safari. He quizzed Dick concerning the quality of trackers Francois had hired for our safari. "Oh, don't you worry. He uses experts from the Wandarobo tribe. They are the best! Some say they can even smell the animals." Will inquired, "Do they use bows or spears to do their personal hunts?" Dick said, "They use both, but they prefer the bow as you do."

Will gave Dick 4,000 shilling to buy a real Maasai spear, shield, and bow. "Oh yes, and please pick out a nice necklace for Jeannie, too." "I'll get your things while I'm up in Northeastern Tanzania on business next week. Arusha is a large enough town that they will have just want you want," Dick said.

Our driver slammed on the van's breaks in front of the small metal building used by our charter air service. As we were getting out, Dick's parting words to us were, "Good luck and be careful. Those animals you are after are dangerous but watch out for the poachers.

They are more dangerous than animals. If you happen on them, in the act of poaching, they'll shoot to kill-and don't often miss!"

The impact of his words ricocheted around in my mind before bursting with full fury on my already rattled nerves. From what Dick had just said, I could very well be picking buck shot out of my backside instead of toasting marshmallows around the campfire! I was out of my comfort zone and wondering what a nice girl like me had gotten myself into???

Drop Off Uncertainties

This time our charter pilot, Chris, was waiting to take us down to the reserve. This tall slender fellow, of Indian descent, spoke perfect English. Will informed Chris that he was a former Alaskan bush pilot, and over the years, he had owned various private planes. He was thrilled when Chris invited him to be his co-pilot. As we strapped ourselves in, Will asked our pilot the distance to the game reserve and a few other pertinent questions. "It's about 190 air miles down to the runway closest to where you'll be hunting." The young pilot asked if Will knew that our campsite, Kibaoni, is the southernmost camp in Tanzania. He knew, but I did not. Will inquired about navigational aids once we left the capital city. This question invoked a chuckle from Chris. "Not a one! No radio beams, no V.O.R.'s (electronic guidance systems), no nothing. Primarily we just follow the rivers." I knew enough pilot's jargon to know what he really meant.

Out here, we fly by the seat of our pants.

Will expressed concern about the current overcast conditions. Chris casually stated, "No problem. There's always quite a lot of cloud cover this time of year, but once we break through the clouds there'll be blue skies above." The two men busied themselves with checking gauges on the instrument panel. Once they felt satisfied that all was in order, Chris made the customary rev-ups, spoke with the control tower, then thrust the gear stick of the heavily loaded Cessna forward. A shiver of apprehension ran up my spine as he opened the throttle and drew the stick back for altitude. We lifted off in hopes of a safe flight and that someone would be there to pick us up once we landed. We were glad to be leaving the petty problems we had encountered in Dar-es-Salaam and could concentrate instead on the adventure that lay ahead at the end of the hour's flight. All the planning for, talking about, and dreaming of, was all behind us now.

If the safari held true to form, by what had already transpired, I surmised our safari was sure to be punctuated by frequent dramas. Some little and some BIG!

We winged our way over the treetops heading due south of the capital city, and sure enough, once we got through the cloud cover, a beautiful sunny day greeted us. As we probed deeper into Tanzania, we swung over ravines and green slopes emerging from the morning haze that they lived in. From this aerial view, I could better understand why the locals preferred the city over this harsh environment where roads were non-existent. The terrain beneath was as unfamiliar to wheels as newborns are to table food.

The closer I got to our destination, the fear of the unknown crept into my mind.

How would it be for a lone woman on safari?

Would the men resent me tagging along?

Would I grow tired of the hunt?

How would I react to conditions in the bush and to the wild animals?

All this and much more remained to be seen.

Chris suddenly banked the plane to the right, causing the shining tips of the plane's wing to slice through a cloud and my heart to jump up in my throat. I had experienced that same awful feeling back in 1979, when our family had survived a twin-engine icing incident that had totaled Will's plane in the Utah desert. His amphibious Grumman Widgeon was one of the few remaining World War II relics still operational. I was not anxious for a repeat performance of our crash landing. It turned out that our sudden change in altitude was due to our pilot's desire to point out the Rufuji River snaking its way through the landscape far below.

Chris yelled to be heard over the noisy engine. "We're on the leading edge of Sand Rivers. The Selous Reserve got this nickname from the natives, because of the two rivers that flow through it."

We flew over old paths stamped out by natives and thirsty animals, until we reached the southernmost leg of the nature refuge. Chris nosed his 402 toward the endless bush canopy on our gradual descent into the depths of elephant country. A parched spot of land in a pocket of arid hills. An occasional tall palm tree poked its head above the trees which became our control tower to help guide us down to earth.

The wheels touched down with a jerk on a desolate primitive dirt runway. After the clouds of dust settled, all I saw was kilometer after kilometer of inhospitable bush country. A place of dysentery, tsetse flies, and malaria.

This was not country for men, but country for elephants, so men come here.

A feeling of skepticism filled every fiber of my being. I inquired of Chris, "How far is it to the nearest town?" He must have read my mind because he laughed at my sudden need to know where the nearest help would come from should we need it. "Jean, I hate to inform you, but nobody lives in or anywhere near the Selous. It is some of the most remote terrain in Africa. Out here you and the wild animals have thousands of square miles all to yourselves."

At this time of the year, the game reserve was extremely dry wearing shades of grey-green, brown tones. The sun lay on it closely causing the ground to feel uncomfortably hot beneath my shoe soles. I likened my reaction of leaving civilization to realizing that the cold reality of winter was upon me, but I was still wearing short sleeves. I stood in the midst of Africa, no longer wondering what it would be like, but with the reality of what it is.

Heaven Help Me!

Chris hurriedly unloaded our belongings, said his goodbyes, then hopped into his shiny passport to civilization and flew off leaving us choking in a whirlwind of dust. Here we stood, in the middle of 'Nowheresville' with no one in sight. With Chris's departure, I experienced the trepidation one has when masked, surgical-nurses wheel you through the doors of the dreaded operating room. There was no doubt about it, we had left civilization.

I was now totally out of my comfort zone.

We were all standing out on the runway clearing, looking around and silently wondering where our guide was, and how long it would be until he arrived. I swallowed hard trying not to look unduly alarmed and desperately hoped that someone knew our whereabouts before the animals sniffed us out. I put on my safari hat to get some relief from the blazing sun, then dug around in my backpack, found the sun block lotion, and liberally applied it onto my sweaty face and arms. The longer I stood on that lonesome runway, the more fear began to overtake me, and I felt as if the trees were closing in on me. I then experienced what being 'scared out of my mind' feels like.

To pass the anxious moments, I put my seldom used marketing degree to work. I occupied my worried mind by conjuring up bizarre ideas that might 'perk-up' the safari outfitters hospitality towards their future clients. The more scared I became, the faster my creative juices flowed, which congealed into some admittedly outrageous ideas. Future visitors might enjoy greetings from drummers beating out welcome messages while monkeys passed out tasty bananas. Or guests might enjoy being serenaded by rhinos tooting their massive horns or lions roaring welcome wishes to the newcomers. New arrivals would also receive valuable coupons distributed from the trunks of adorable elephants. Each enticing offer was designed to lure tourist into the huts of local entrepreneurs:

<u>Coupon 1</u>: Hungry Hippo Bar-B-Q!! Half off-Wart Hog Sandwiches, smothered in green mamba snake sauce, topped with velcheetah cheese, on a fire toasted bun + FREE bottle of flavor-infused River Water!

<u>Coupon 2</u>: World-class wrestling, featuring "Carlos the Cremator", appearing at the Laughing Hyena Arena. Catch every thrilling match as Carlos crushes all competitors. FREE medical assistance to those who challenge this unbeaten champion!

<u>Coupon 3</u>: Join a head-butting contest with 'Bruno, the Bonehead!' This Cape Buffalo leaves a literal impression on his opponents. Bruno's mind-blowing cranial adjustments-NO extra charge!'

My creative delusions occupied my mind for what seemed like an eternity. Suddenly, hope became a reality. Off in the distance, we noticed a rust-colored dust cloud moving steadily towards us. I was unsure whether to jump for joy or run for cover?

Was it our white hunter, poachers, or a herd of stampeding animals?

Chapter 6

Heading to Main Camp

Out of the dust cloud emerged, 'a sight for sore eyes', two dusty green Land Rovers. Both jeeps unloaded their passengers. One white man, a veteran of the African bush for 18 years, and the rest natives wearing skin as black as coal. In his beautiful French accent, Francois introduced himself as our hunting guide. My idea of what he should look like did not coincide with his appearance. He wore a pair of well-worn, ill-fitting khaki pants, a limp green cloth hat, and a pair of dusty athletic shoes. His sun faded green shirt, with a sizable tear on one shoulder, caused me to wonder who or what had caused that??

Francois introduced his black entourage consisting of a game scout, a government representative, drivers, mechanics, and three trackers. The latter wore solid green pants and matching shirts. Francois singled out the oldest man. While patting him on the back, he said with great admiration, "This is Kisenga, our head tracker."

When Francois wanted the best, he hired this ebony-tinted tracker. Although he had gained considerable notoriety, Kisenga had not let fame go to his head, but preferred living amongst his people in comparative anonymity.

Kisenga's most distinguishing feature was the large holes that members of his tribe purposely make in their earlobes.

A tall, young man named Rembeo was Francois' personal tracker, and Zuberi, a shorter, younger man, was hired as assistant tracker. These experts brought with them inordinately keen eyes and the tracking instincts of a bloodhound. Throughout our safari they continually demonstrated these amazing abilities. Francois told Will, "I hand-picked these seasoned hunting experts for your special bow safari. They belong to the Wandarobo tribe, which hails from Tanzania's northernmost region. This tribe hunts with the bow as you do, but the difference is they have government approval to use poisonous arrows and spears to bring down their game."

The remainder of Francois' staff wore an eclectic assortment of clothing given to them by previous hunters. In view of the intense heat, I was amazed at how much clothing these natives wore.

How would I look, to the outside world, after 21 days in the wilds of Africa?

When the time seemed appropriate, I handed Francois the package Mrs. Pasanisi had sent him. It contained Will's government approval to take a specified number of designated animals. Also, in the package was a medication that would, hopefully, alleviate the severe headaches Francois was experiencing from recent malaria flare-ups. Janine had indicated to me, "Francois has sufficient malaria in his system to prove the undoing of ten ordinary men. Every now and again his malaria attacks him, but don't worry, he'll perform his job with his usual competence." He opened it, took several pills, and washed them down with a bottle of soda pop.

Janine also included a letter, which he eagerly tore open. He removed his hat and began reading. He was hungrily devouring its contents to the degree that I was surprised that the ink stayed on the page. Once out from underneath his hat and sunglasses, I realized how handsome he was. Francois looked like a swarthy French model and was decidedly 'eye candy.' The length of his sun-bleached blond hair and the depth of his tan indicated that he had been away from civilization for an extended period of time.

My trip around the world suddenly seemed more palatable, whether I saw an animal or not!

I asked Will if there was a toilet at this isolated airstrip. My husband confirmed my suspicions that no such convenience existed out here. Wearing a big grin, he pointed toward the brush, "Jeannie, pick out and get behind the tree of your choice." Francois saw me wandering off from the group and asked where I was going. I told him. "Okay, then don't go far. We've recently spotted lions in the vicinity."

I will never know if he was serious, but with his 'lions lurking nearby' comment foremost in my mind, I made a world record 'pit stop!' The Indy 500 crews would have been astonished at how quickly I made it out of the bush and back to our group.

Upon my return, Francois offered us a soft drink from the insulated box in the back of one of the rigs. Although lukewarm, this cola hit the spot on such a sweltering day.

Francois then said to Will, "We're anxious to see how good you are with your bow."

Will obliged his onlookers, by assembling his archery equipment. Brian and Denny readied the filming apparatus to record everyone's reaction to Will's archery expertise. It was a proud moment when Will showed off his amazing shooting abilities to his skeptical audience. It was obvious that they were duly impressed. During the 'show and tell' exhibition, I used the time to make some notes about our trip to Sand Rivers.

Soon two additional jeeps arrived. We quickly loaded up and our safari expedition set out for the lengthy trip to the main camp in our hunting district. I was fortunate to have been sandwiched in between Francois on my left, one of Africa's premier game experts, and Will on my right, an extraordinary archer and outdoorsman. From this vantage point, I became privy to what was taking place, as well as their interesting stories and conversations. Whenever possible during our time together, I enjoyed listening to Francois' incredible stories about his experiences in Africa.

Our trackers, Kisenga, Rembeo, and Zuberi stood directly behind us in the open-topped jeep. These natives were exceptional at spotting game, which for a non-hunter like me, was virtually impossible. I was flabbergasted at how difficult even the large game was to spot.

Their coloring and habitat camouflaged them from a casual observer like me. Usually, I could only see them when they were on the move.

Brian and Denny's jeep followed behind our rig. They planned it that way, so they would be in a position to film any action. While on the dirt trails, they had to eat our dust, but fortunately most of the safari took place as we drove up and down the sandy river bottoms. The road was extremely bumpy and occasionally quite steep. It was necessary to stand up and use our legs as shock absorbers as we held on tightly to the jeep's roll bar.

I had brought along a hat that I had purchased from a well-known safari outfitter. My traditional khaki colored pith helmet was the cherry on top of my chic safari attire. In theory, it looked good, but its Achilles heel was-no chin strap.

The big city designers had obviously never left their offices to test their creation in real life conditions. I suspected that the closest thing they had been to a safari situation was riding the outside escalators at the San Diego Zoo.

Whenever the jeep sped up, the least bit of wind caused my hat to blow off. Three times the driver patiently backed up and one of the workers hopped out and picked it up. Francois put an end to our time-consuming 'fetching' by reaching underneath his seat, pulling something out; then quickly placing it behind his back. While wearing a big smile, he surprised me by snatching the pith helmet off my head and replacing it with an old dusty baseball cap. I was already beginning to look like one of the 'wandering robo' tribe But I will say this, for the tacky hat, it never blew off. And, by the way, I never saw that hideous helmet again.

I was no longer the poster girl for Abercrombie and Fitch.

Our caravan slowed as we passed through the remnants of the patrol station. It's decaying boards and rusting tin roof looked suspiciously at us as if to question our intentions for entering this private animal haven. A place richly endowed by God and untouched by mankind that a spiritual feeling came over me as if I had entered the Garden of Eden.

Francois began telling us about safaris of the past. "Years ago, we used an entourage of porters who carried everything, and I might add, much of it atop their heads. One hunter insisted on bringing his creature comforts along, so three men carried his bathtub through the bush. Back then, we would walk between 20 and 40 kilometers per day. We carried our own pack, a map, and a compass. Conditions were more primitive then, and it might take us twelve days to walk the 155 miles."

I got excited as we began seeing a diverse range of wildlife: warthogs, zebras, antelopes, Jackals, hippos, Cape buffalo, and several of the 350 species of birds. When we passed by several large monkeys, Francois said, "The natives nicknamed the baboons *politicians*."

We all knew some elected officials who aptly fitted that description, so his comment elicited a big laugh from everyone.

Uncovering this primordial world melted my inhibitions about being on safari like snow on a warm spring day. My heart expanded with a wondrous sense of privilege. Everywhere I looked there was something new and exciting; similar to watching an action packed, 3-ring circus. I thoroughly enjoyed our fascinating journey into one of the largest remaining wilderness areas in Africa.

Our knowledgeable guide began unfolding the remarkable history of how this immense sanctuary came to be. "The locals call the reserve Sand Rivers because its rivers are one of the most unique features of the Selous landscape. Over the years, this territory has grown from 1,000 to 21,100 square miles, which is twice as large as your state of Maryland. It has a wide range of natural resources, and more than 2,100 plants have been recorded.

As early as 1922, the British established this reserve. It is named after Frederick Courteney Selous, an English naturalist, elephant hunter, and explorer. You Americans may be interested to know that Selous, a very sought-after individual, was a white hunter to your President Theodore Roosevelt. Starting in 1871, Selous spent 40 years gaining extensive knowledge of the wilderness. According to historians, the British were engaged in a squabble with German forces over who would control this vital bush country. In 1917 Selous was mortally wounded by a German sniper during the Brits advance to the Rufuji River. A white rectangular concrete marker was erected in the reserve on the spot where he died."

Francois went on to reiterate, "Other great individuals also helped mold the reserve into what it is today-a self-perpetuating bastion of African wilderness where animals wander in merciful ignorance of human beings. One such person was C.J.P. Ionides, a precocious conservationist who became its savior, hence, his title- 'Father of the Selous.' He went by his nickname 'Iodine.' For 20 years, he devoted his boundless energies to exploring and mapping the region on foot in his position as a game ranger."

I remarked to Francois, "Chris our pilot told me that there are no humans living in or around the reserve. Why is that?" He explained, "The scattered villagers were moved out in 1936, precipitated by an outbreak of sleeping sickness caused by the abundant tsetse fly population. This is coupled with the fact that it became humanly impossible, for 'Iodine's' limited staff, to protect the populace living here from the large elephant population. These mammals repeatedly inflicted serious damage on the tribes isolated small villages, houses, and crops. The colonial government faced with a pretty bleak situation, finally concluded that the Ionides' inspired policy of denying all protection to the natives living in the Selous, was the only sensible solution. In 1943, the last of the Ngindo tribesmen moved to settlements outside the controlled area. Once gone, the territory was declared by the government, a game sanctuary, making resettlement illegal. All settlements are now located quite a distance outside these sprawling boundaries. Consequently, in the southern region where we are, the areas around the Selous are as uninhabited as the reserve itself. Before the beloved Ionides was finished, the reserve had been enlarged 20 times.

By 1951, the main outlines of the Selous were established by law. Important additions were subsequently made by Brian Nicholson who served as a game warden here for some 20 years. What most people do not realize is that today our reserve is four times larger than the more famous Serengeti National Park, which lies on the Kenyan border in northern Tanzania. Our beautiful, well-organized game paradise supports more than 100,000 elephants, along with lions, leopards, huge herds of Cape buffalo, hippos, and numerous antelope species-just to name a few. This is not a national park but is the greatest stronghold of large wild animal life on Earth!

Tanzanian policy dictates that invited visitors hunting the reserve pay for game managers to supervise their safari around-the-clock. This ensures that the reserve's rules are strictly adhered to. The restrictions are intended to stop the indiscriminate killing of females and young, plus the unlawful sale of meat, skins, and ivory.

A game scout named Manyimancu, and Edmond, an English-speaking native from the Tanzanian Wildlife Corporation, were the officials chosen to accompany our safari. These wild game specialists proved to be invaluable throughout our hunt. Game quotas in the reserve are set by experts for each hunting block, thus making it possible to maintain the proper ecological balance according to the food available in each area. All animals taken, whether for camp meat, bait, or trophy, are accounted and paid for by the hunter. Any kill made by any member of our group would also count toward Will's hunting limit."

Francois then enthusiastically stated, "We are in the real African bush as it has existed for thousands of years." Francois then stated, "Because your bow hunt is a dangerous project, seldom done before, we will have to stalk the animals at close range. There is no doubt that this type of hunt will be much more dangerous than a rifle hunt could ever be!"

Too Close for Comfort

As we traveled toward the main camp, we had what Francois termed as a rare occurrence. We happened upon six African men making the 100-mile journey across the wildlife sanctuary on their way to another settlement. Francois informed us, "The foot path they're on connects the village of Konga on the northwest of the reserve to Liwale on the east." We stopped for a visit and found these natives very friendly. Each was dressed in a long, wrap-round skirt wearing a unique and, frankly, comical, homespun hat.

If I did not know better, I would say they were in costume heading for the T.V. show 'Let's Make A Deal.'

It concerned me that these men had to walk such long distances with no means of protecting themselves from the wild animals. Francois later explained, "As a safeguard to the animals, no one without a permit can carry weapons in the reserve. The natives must stay on the paths. Since poaching is rife, it is assumed that those not on the path are up to no good. The malicious poachers are so dangerous that game managers have learned from experience to shoot first and ask questions later."

As the travelers chattered amongst themselves it became obvious, from their body language, that they were intrigued by Will's archery equipment. Noticing their fascination, Will placed one of his bows into their hard-working hands and said, "Francois, tell them to try to pull the bow." Each made a valiant attempt, but none of them succeeded in pulling it. We were amazed at how good natured they remained while struggling to budge the powerful bow.

In retrospect, these natives were the only humans we encountered in the game sanctuary, except for those directly connected with the safari. We were so far off the beaten path that the only outside reminder of civilization came one afternoon when I heard the faint sound of an airplane engine way off in the distance.

There are few places left on earth where one could have been so isolated. No zip codes, no parking meters, no pizza deliveries, no power poles, no emergency sirens, no TV, no Girl Scout cookie sales, no smog-just fascinating wildlife abounding everywhere.

My stomach was growling when Francois finally stopped the driver for a lunch break. We picnicked underneath a huge shade tree close to a beautiful *mkondo*, or stream. For comfort, the jeep's terry cloth covered cushions were removed and placed on the ground for us to sit on. Although we were out in the middle of nowhere, Francois brought out a large wicker picnic basket. He laid before us a linen tablecloth matching napkins, flatware, plates, and food. I was shocked at this unexpected touch of class.

I was thinking that he might also produce a candelabra, but it never appeared.

The Black personnel, except Edmond, ate nearby underneath a separate tree. Throughout the hunt, Edmond, the black TAWICO representative, ate with us. His position in the government and his educational background had placed him in a category apart from his fellow compatriots. His clothing was nicer, and he spoke fluent English. His mannerisms were more refined, and we enjoyed his company and the interesting information he shared about the animals he was entrusted with protecting. I was glad to see that his mixing with us did not engender any animosity amongst his fellow countrymen.

While relaxing, I asked Francois to tell us about some unique individuals he had guided over the years. I sat spellbound as he related, in his beautiful French accent, a story about an elderly woman who was on safari here in the Selous. He began by looking over at me, "She was a woman too. But not at all like you. She was a wealthy widow and old, 70, 75, and frail. She walked haltingly, but never bent over. She walked tall, straight, and with dignity.

Everywhere we went I guided her, like a princess, on my arm. Whenever I spotted a Cape buffalo we would stop. I would lift her out of the vehicle and prop her heavy rifle up against the hood. Then lean her up against the jeep where she would take aim, and shoot." I asked, "Was she able to hit the buffalo?" Francois emphatically stated, "Always! She was a crack shot. Good eyes. Good aim. Good luck."

Will asked Edmond if he would help him understand more about an elephant's ivory. Edmond agreed, "Well, back in the 50's, elephants had bigger tusks. Their 'white gold' averaged around 8 feet in length." Francois swallowed his bite of food and added, "The best bull's ivory I ever personally took was a 130 pounder. Then added for clarification "That is 130 per tusk! I found him in the big forests north of Tanzania and Kenya."

Francois added, "Their tusks are actually just long carved upper teeth, called incisors, made of ivory. After the baby milk tusk stage, these extensions grow throughout the animal's life. They are much longer than they appear. Very few people know that only two-thirds of each tusk extend from the upper jaw; the remainder rests inside the skull." Francois passed around the rolls and continued talking about his beloved elephants. "Under good conditions, their tusks gain a couple of pounds each year. But I know that is not always the case, because I see old, old bulls that are obviously on their last legs, and they have only got 30 to 40 pounds of ivory. But then you will see another one at that age with tusks weighing 100 pounds. To me, it is not a cut and dried situation. Personally, good incisors stem from genetic makeup and the kind of minerals they get in their diet." Between mouthfuls he concluded by saying, "Those tusks weigh as much as 1 short ton and that ain't hay!"

After lunch, Brian went over to the *mkondo,* stream, to relieve himself behind a tree. While there, he had a completely unexpected and downright terrifying experience. While Brian had his back turned to the creek, a huge Cape buffalo came out of the bush close to where he stood. Realizing his life was in jeopardy, the cameraman tried making his 210-pound frame invisible. When that did not pan out, he ever so slowly maneuvered himself around his 'pee tree' to get out of the buffalo's sight. When he felt it was safe to do so, Brian fled from the ominous, heavily horned bull, the way a man with longer legs and fewer inches around his waist would run.

All heads jerked around when we heard, then saw, our cameraman storming towards us as if his hair were on fire. We knew, before being told, that our camera buff had just experienced something quite traumatic. After explaining to us what had just happened, he blurted out from his pale sweaty face "I'm NEVER going to be caught again without my Smith & Wesson Magnum .44 pistol that I brought for this trip."

Francois told Brian, "I hate to tell you, but your pistol is useless here. That handgun does not have the 'oomph' needed to bring down any of the thick hided African animals. But if carrying it makes you feel more comfortable then be my guest." Will flippantly followed with, "Hey Brian, hang on to your pistol, it might come in handy to commit suicide in case you get attacked."

I got the distinct impression that Brian, having just been at death's door, did not appreciate Will's uncalled for wisecrack. Neither Will nor Denny had even bothered bringing a gun to Africa. I had never owned a gun. The only thing I had ever shot was a water gun and a spitball wad at a substitute teacher's back in Junior High School.

Our entire safari party had to depend on Francois, Edmond, and Manyimancu for protection. Will was always with Francois, who was never without his custom .460 caliber bolt-action rifle, the best and most powerful rifle on the market. Edmond protected the camera crew, and I stuck close to Manyimancu the game scout assigned to guard me.

Before long, the jeeps left the dusty, bumpy road and began traveling down the middle of the sandy M'barangandu River bottom. It was a hot day and occasionally we ran into pockets of pesky tsetse flies.

After all our dreaming about and planning for the safari, I was not about to let temporary inconveniences dampen my enthusiasm. I just concentrated on the fact that I was the only woman for miles in the midst of the finest wildlife habitat in Africa!

We had not gone far before our trackers spotted a lone bull elephant and uttered the word we had come so far to hear– *'TEMBO'!* The bull was packing at least 60 lbs. or more of ivory on each side. I caught sight of the hindquarter of this unmatched symbol of the African wild as it disappeared over the crest of a nearby hill. His tusks were sufficiently sizeable that Francois and Will thought it best to take a closer look.

Excitement filled the air, like a movie set: Elephant–Camera– Action!

Will grabbed his fiberglass bow and a handful of the specialty arrows he had developed for hunting elephant. Denny, our sound man, hovered over Will and Francois attaching lavaliere microphones which would record the conversations between the stars of our show. In jest, Denny instructed Will, "Just ignore this mike. It'll pick up everything, just don't say anything you don't want Jeannie to hear."

Francois and Will stormed up the steep embankment followed by a trail of men and one very curious woman close on their heels. I reached the top of the hill out of breath and panting heavily. I was glad that prior to the hunt I had prepared myself physically for just such an occasion. We followed behind our unsuspecting six-ton *tembo* who soon met up with one of his cronies. Now we had to deal with two mammoth beasts. Will and Francois took the lead. Denny and Brian followed behind at about 40 yards. I stayed back with the trackers another 30 yards and watched the action through my binoculars. Up ahead I could see the arrows jostling up and down inside the brown leather quiver between Will's bare shoulder blades.

After a while, the elephants stopped, in a grove of trees, and began munching on some leaves. These pachyderms, whose insatiable appetites are matched only by their size, require all the food they can find. Their lengthy trunks help them exploit every food source. This unique appendage even allows them to reach as high in the treetops as long-necked giraffes. The enormous hindquarters of the two bulls loomed before me like grey boulders welling up from the earth.

Francois suddenly stopped and whispered with his fingers. Will responded to his prearranged signal and moved in slowly. It took over an hour for Francois to skillfully maneuver his client into position for a shot only 20 paces from his intended target. It was then that the anxious archer made a very foolish decision. Will determined that for his shot to get maximum penetration he should move to within 10 yards of the bull. I watched my mate inch ever closer to his demise. I could not begrudge my husband his big moment, but I sure wanted to.

From years of dealing with elephants, Francois knew their disposition can change, like the wind, from one moment to the next. Will's present distance was now much too close. Francois tried to get his client to retreat. Sure enough, the overconfident, neophyte elephant hunter was in BIG trouble! In the blink of an eye, the elephant's demeanor suddenly changed. He had obviously grazed over a patch of grass where Will had previously been and picked up human scent. Like all elephants, he did not possess keen eyesight, but he was adroit at following scent and sound until he could find his culprit. This bull had Will's whereabouts pegged. The alerted bull raised his head, lifted his trunk, then turned all 12,000 precocious pounds abruptly toward Will. My heart pounded in alarm! Will remained frozen in his tracks with the inconspicuous eye of the camera upon his precarious situation. There they were-man and beast-the bothered bull and unwavering Will.

As we watched the traumatic standoff this thought passed through my mind. Here stands either a brave man or one with suicidal tendencies.

I began noticing that my spouse was undergoing some sort of a metamorphosis in preparation for meeting his Maker. Will's face took on an arrogant expression. His steel blue eyes were squinted and appeared glazed over. His neck muscles looked extended and swollen like the neck of an angry snake. Beads of sweat ran down his face which turned into white froth at the corners of his mouth. His stance was rigid as he stared up in defiance at his gigantic opponent who stood a good 12 feet high at the shoulders. The bull's gargantuan ears were spread open, 'as BIG as Texas,' as if to capture even the sound of our breathing. Those outstretched ears made the bull appear even more ominous. As I watched this surreal, terrifying event unfolding before my eyes, I grabbed Kisenga's arm and squeezed a silent scream. He did not take his eyes off the big bull but nodded that he knew I was silently freaking out and needed support. It was sheer agony watching Earth's biggest land animal about to charge my husband.

This was too much for Francois, who was responsible for his client's wellbeing. In his most authoritative voice, he loudly hailed Will to "MOVE BACK." At the same instant, he fired several rounds over the elephant's head.

Denny, who was wearing headphones, recording the situation, came a good foot off the ground and was temporarily deafened by the unexpected ear-piercing gun blasts. I was so far back I could not see exactly what had transpired. I shut my eyes praying that I had not been clairvoyant the morning we left home in my snide remark about bringing Will's remains back home. Immense relief flooded over me as I saw everyone heading in my direction.

Having no preconceived notions about what to expect on safari was good and bad. I just took things as they came and dealt with them on the spot. If I had known about the dangers, remoteness, and hardships that I would encounter, chances are I would have stayed home. But I would have never experienced Africa in its raw state, never witnessed the amazing animals, and never written about our safari from a women's viewpoint.

After the excitement, we gathered back at the jeeps and continued towards Kibaoni. After a while, Francois halted our caravan atop a hill. We peered down upon our picturesque campsite on the banks of the M'barangandu River, where daily thousands of animals came to drink from its life-giving waters.

I wondered if the English translation of M'barangandu might be 'river of no return.' This was our first day in the reserve and both Brian and Will had almost lost their lives. I dared not think about what perils might be in store for us once the safari began in earnest.

Buffalo Business

Upon our arrival at the main camp, a sizable staff lined up to greet us outside a large tent, which served as the camp's nucleus. We gave the customary welcome greeting '*Jambo*' to cooks, porters, laundry personnel, servers, storekeepers, tent boys, drivers, mechanics, etc. We were invited inside the spacious tent to relax and enjoy a cold drink to help refresh us after our long ride and trek in the bush.

Life at Kibaoni was not as uncivilized as I had expected. Occupying the center space in the tent was a circular table which could seat twelve. It was set with everything from linens to wine glasses. I never fathomed that this remote camp would be equipped with an electric refrigerator and chest type freezer. Two native, English-speaking, servers in white jackets attended to our every need. Our safari party was fortunate indeed because a last-minute cancellation meant we had the entire hunting section, camp facilities and staff all to ourselves.

Rama, one of the servers, greeted me by saying, "Welcome to camp *Mama Mshale*."

Why did he call me by that name?

Francois smiled and explained, "In Swahili '*mama*' means mother and '*mshale*' is arrow. He is saying that you are the 'mother of the arrow' or in English 'the archer's wife'." From that point on, I became known as '*Mama Mshale*' and Will was '*Big Bwana.* '

Francois excused himself and left the tent. A brief time later he nonchalantly sauntered in, smiled, and seated himself directly across the table from me. He had bathed, spruced himself up, and was no longer in his old, torn clothing. I tried not to make an audible gasp at his remarkable transformation into 'Cinderfellow'! The sleeves of his white shirt were rolled up. Several of the top buttons on his shirt were open revealing his suntanned muscular chest. He completed his 'killer' look with a dark blue, silk neck scarf and a pair of tight fitting, well-worn blue jeans. He was now clean shaven and had slicked his long hair back. He resembled a sexy model used by Haute couture fashion designers to entice women into purchasing their exclusive clothing and fragrances.

Who could have imagined my luck at having this handsome 'hunk' to look at for 3 long weeks in the wilds of Africa?

Later Francois escorted us to our tent where our belongings had been put. This canvas abode was one of the old-style, green Manyara tents with its traditional rain fly. It had been erected underneath two large shade trees. Inside our quarters, there were twin beds separated by a small wooden table. Our housing was austere, but immaculate.

Francois told us, "Discard your dirty laundry on the floor each day, When Japhet cleans your tent each morning, he'll wash and iron them for you." Since we could only bring a few changes of clothing, our laundry service was an unexpected luxury. Sure enough, each evening when we returned, we found clean, neatly ironed, folded clothing on our beds.

I wanted to clone Japhet and take him home to help with the piles of laundry our family generated daily.

Outside our tent, a table had been skillfully lashed together. On it were drinking glasses, individual water basins, and a mirror. I was not sure I was going to like my reflection as makeup, hair dryers, and curling irons were out of the question. From now on, I just washed, and towel dried my hair, put on sun block, and hit the road. The camp's guests shared two outdoor shower stalls and an outdoor toilet. The workers had erected sturdy dry grass enclosures around each convenience. Although there were electric lights installed inside the tents, showers, and on the water stands, the electricity was unreliable due to an antiquated generator. During the frequent outages, Francois suggested we resort to our *'torches,'* flashlights.

It was comforting to learn that the main camp was equipped with a two-way radio.

Our safari leader suggested that we use the remaining daylight to clean up for dinner. "Whenever you want to shower, just yell *magi ya moto*, hot water. The words sounded Japanese, but every time I uttered them a water boy came running with a bucket full of warm water, which he dumped into a long canvas bag. This showering devise was then raised or lowered, depending on one's height, over a tree limb inside the shower enclosure. To release the water, I turned a control spigot attached to the end of the bag. This little apparatus made life bearable after a long hot day in the bush.

After showering, we dressed and gathered in the mess tent. For our first night in camp the head chef had prepared *kongoni*, which had been left over from a previous client's hunt. I was ravenous, but a bit skeptical as to how the antelope would taste. It was surprisingly tender, deliciously prepared, and very tasty. At dinner, I learned that the hunter must provide the camp's meat supply. Since we were on a bow hunt, I savored every morsel surmising that our meat-eating days were about over.

After the dishes were cleared, our server, John, leaned over and said, "Excuse me madam, have you brought along any painkillers?" I looked up and noticed, for the first time, that his left cheek was badly swollen. One of his molars was badly infected and in need of medical attention. I excused myself to get what he needed from the medical supplies we had brought with us. We had come prepared for whatever minor medical issues might arise. Hopefully, we would not need to use them, but it was reassuring to know that we had them should they be needed. I handed John his pain meds, for which he was grateful.

Will and Francois began looking at maps of the area and discussing where they intended to hunt and what animals would be in those locations. Francois pointed at the map saying, "Right here, I recently saw the remains of a lion that a Cape buffalo had killed with his heavy hooves and horns." Denny remarked, "I've heard that each year hippos kill many people in Africa." Francois nodded in agreement. "Yes, lots of them. This is the animal we have got to be careful of. Most are short, 3½ feet in height, which does not seem formidable, but their hefty weight of between one and two tons makes them a fearsome adversary. And that is not taking into consideration their massive mouths, which are 4 feet across and full of huge ivory teeth."

When Will had seen and heard enough, we excused ourselves and walked a short distance to our tent. I wanted to discuss the day's traumatic events and was anxious to know what was going through his mind when the elephant was about to charge. I wished to express how worried I had been and how glad I was that he was not killed. My husband, eleven years my senior, was either too exhausted or his male ego would not allow him to own up to the fact that his poor judgment had almost gotten himself killed. He dodged my enquires by yawning and crawling into bed. I dug around in my bag, found the family picture, and placed it on the small table between us. I knelt and thanked the good Lord that Francois had saved me from being a widow and many other things. Then I stopped for the day too.

And what a memorable day it had been!! I was wound up, like a 400-day clock, and unable to relax enough to fall asleep. I was too high on Africa and all that I had experienced. It was surprising that Africa exhilarated rather than irritated me.

For the longest time, I lay there listening to the sounds of wild animals roaming near our encampment. The one that worried me the most was making low mournful grunts. Eventually, I fell asleep to the monotonous noise of crickets, which sounded like the snipping of barber scissors at a military base preparing inductees for boot camp.

The next morning, I was awakened by fresh water being poured into my enamel washbasin. I moved. I stretched. I opened my eyes and focused on the outline of our tent.

Where was I? Oh, yes, in Africa!

A chorus of noisy birds chirped happily overhead. The aroma from a fire drifted my direction, which meant the cook was in the process of preparing our breakfast. Will had already dressed and was gone. I anxiously climbed into my crisp new safari clothing then went outside to wash up. The warm water felt invigorating and helped wake me up. The men were in the dining tent, deep in a discussion of their plans for the day. The servers explained that I could order my eggs the way I liked, but the remainder of the meal was the cook's choice.

After breakfast, Will and Denny busied themselves down on the river bottom, fine-tuning the archery equipment, and practice shooting. This gave me a chance to organize my backpack for the day's outing. I began packing pencil, sharpener, journal, sunglasses, tissues, lipstick, sun block, dental floss, hand sanitizer, binoculars, hat, insect repellant, hairbrush, nail file, collapsible cup, water jug, bandages, aspirin, camera, batteries, extra film, energy powders, camo jacket, and tsetse fly protective clothing. I was hopefully ready for whatever action would come my way.

With my remaining time, I explored our large campsite. While heading down toward the river, I passed several large tents which housed the workers. I walked past the skinner's work area. Many of the animal skulls, horns, and tusks, had been placed up on a thatched area to dry in the sun. The trophies, I was told, must dry out before being shipped throughout the world to their respective owners. It was comforting to know that these animals had been culled under strict supervision, nevertheless, I was still uncomfortable with the killing aspect of a safari.

My binoculars came in handy to view the many animals gathered to quench their theist from the small amount of water still visible along the opposite bank. I watched it enthralled by their fascinating behavior. All to soon I heard the jeep engines warming up, which I correctly assumed indicated our immanent departure.

While getting seated in the jeep, a flock of Egyptian geese gracefully hovered overhead in the clear blue sky. This was especially thrilling to Denny, the bird watcher amongst us. This sighting gave him another species to add to his ever-growing list of birds. Wildlife viewing was equally spectacular downstream. We saw numerous large gatherings of antelope at the river's edge. Francois pointed out a sickly looking one amongst them. "That puny runt won't last long out here," he muttered under his breath with a foreboding sound in his voice. "Why not? It has lots of company to protect it." Francois explained to me, "But that doesn't deter the hungry lions and other predators who are constantly looking to take down any weak animal."

The close calls that Brian and Will had already experienced, coupled with Francois' statement, gave added credence to just how dangerous this place was for man and beast.

We had not traveled far when we saw, on the horizon, a dark mass of animals. It was several hundred Cape buffalo standing in a compact herd staring back at our convoy. It was evident that if we ventured too close and disturbed this heavy-horned herd, we would be in danger of being trampled to death.

Francois told Will, "We need to find some lone bulls for your bow. Chances are there will be some upstream." Sure enough, we happened on several large Cape buffalo which had separated themselves from the herd. These big bulls were exactly what Francois had hoped to find. They were standing near the left bank up ahead, blissfully unaware that they were being sized up as potential target.

Our white hunter's job was to produce the desired game and point it out to his client. Together they would gauge the animal's size, its immediate intentions, and strategic disposition. Then, and only then, would the stalk begin.

Once Will gave Francois the thumbs-up signal, everyone gathered their belongings and hopped out of the jeeps to begin the stalking. The men politely enquired, "*Mama,* would you prefer to wait in the jeep?" I thanked them for their kind offer but indicated that it would be impossible for me to write about things I had not witnessed firsthand.

I thought to myself that I had not come all this way to 'cool my heels' in some jeep.

I too jumped out, grabbed my backpack, and hoped I could keep pace with the men. "Be careful Jean," Denny whispered. "Cape buffalos are noted for having a bad temper. They are not like the buffalos in India you see plowing the fields. These bruisers are definitely not domesticated." I smiled indicating that I understood.

But did I really?

Kisenga, considered by his peers as elderly at the ripe old age of 45, took the lead and skillfully guided us through the bush. He had kind brown eyes. His wrinkled face, from years of sun exposure, resembled a well-cured nut. We were in awe of this veteran's tracking prowess. It was a pleasure to watch him at his work. His ability to move stealthily through the bush was an art that he had perfected over many years. His technique was not a matter of watching where he stepped, but rather keeping his eyes riveted on the place where he wanted to be.

As we walked, we talked quietly amongst ourselves until we reached the trees. From this point on our safari personnel's demeanor drastically changed. Everything slowed down to a snail's pace and many times the trackers stopped to double-check the situation. It was obvious that these men took their jobs very seriously and for good reason, anything could be lurking up ahead. We moved in single file through the bush for the longest time, then Kisenga suddenly halted us, and all eyes followed his eyes.

He was staring into some brush up ahead. Much to my surprise, he had brought Will out at the precise opening on the bank where he needed to be. The unsuspecting Cape buffalo stood in the riverbed just 25 yards from Will's position. It appeared, from my vantage point, that he was so close that he could have counted the hairs on his back. With hands, steady as a rock, Will hurriedly notched one of his arrows and, with all his might, let it fly. The shot entered the buffalo's massive rib cage and subsequently we heard breaking bones. The startled buffalo took off running. The trackers followed the blood trail which, at times, was difficult to locate.

Edmond told me, "*Mama* you'd best stay put under this tree while the men search for the dangerous wounded buffalo." While they were consumed with tracking, I sat down to capture these exciting events in my journal. The men became so engrossed in locating the bull's trail that I completely lost sight of them.

After a while Will realized that I was missing and came to get me. He said, "Jean, I was worried about you. It's obvious you don't realize the jeopardy you are in. I'll get you back to the group. Please be super careful from now on and stay close to Manyimancu. Francois just instructed him to keep you safe." After several hours, the men successfully spotted a small section of the buffalo's rump sticking out of some dry weeds, where it was attempting to recuperate. The good news was his resting meant he was probably mortally wounded. The bad news was the wounded animal had spotted us long before we had caught sight of him.

"Be quiet, *Mama*, and don't move," were Francois' whispered words of warning. We made no sound and tried to mimic mannequins while being totally exposed in the middle of an open expanse. I was also worried because the terrain underfoot would be impossible to run on in the event we needed to do so. The hard, dried earth was full of deep holes made by large animals during the rainy season. Our safari leader looked more concerned than usual as he silently signaled a retreat for cover.

His hand was tightly clutching his rifle, like an eagle clinging to a tree branch in a windstorm.

As we slowly retreated, all eyes watched the dangerous animal, which could at any moment decide to charge us from his 'sick bay.' Once we were out of the bull's sight, Will slowly inched his way forward, but because there was no cover, he was not able to get close enough to make a clean shot. All he could see through the weeds was a small fraction of the bull's hindquarter. Bow drawn, he released. The razor-sharp blades went through its hairy hide and lodged somewhere inside.

The twice wounded bruiser immediately sprang to his feet. We were surprised to see there were two other buffalos accompanying him. We heard their hooves mowing down the deep grass as they went bursting through the bush using their thick horns to clear an escape route. Will told Francois, "I'm wondering why my second shot didn't drop him after he ran a hundred yards or so." "You probably just hit him in the hip," was Francois' deduction, "but part of our problem is the fact that his companions are encouraging him to keep going."

This was an admirable thing to do for their dying friend.

We followed the trackers to a place beyond one of the ravines where the wounded animal had once again rested. The trackers searched high and low in and around that ravine, and finally located a small blood sign indicating he had pushed off elsewhere. We followed and later found another place where the buffalo had laid down, but his bleeding had all but stopped. Francois consoled his discouraged client, "There is a good chance that we'll lose him now, because if he's able to get up that hill, it means he is strong. He is hurt, but not so badly that he can't travel for a while. But don't despair because quite often we can recover them. They won't go as far as an elephant. If you get a bad hit on them, chances are you'll lose him."

It was then that we became painfully aware of the undeniable fact that the sun would soon be setting, and we would be left in the bush with a wounded Cape buffalo on the loose, one whose disposition would worsen, if surprised. On top of that, if we did not get back to the waiting vehicles, we would be groping around in the dark since no one had brought along a flashlight. As we hustled back to our transportation, I heard Francois saying to his dejected client, "During the night your lethal broadheads will have more time to work and we will probably find him dead tomorrow.

Chapter 7

Treacherous Tracking

We walked for miles as fast as our legs could carry us. Just at dark we reached the safety of our vehicles. I was utterly exhausted and starving from a demanding day of non-stop chasing a hairy, heavy-horned beast. With my last ounce of energy, I climbed up into the jeep and we headed for 'home' beneath a canopy of brilliant stars.

Our discussion about the day's events abruptly ended when Francois spotted something worrisome. He told the driver to stop and hand him the torch. Sure enough, his keen eyes had picked up several *simbas,* lions, cooling their bellies on the moist sand. In the piercing scrutiny of his flashlight, these powerful animals appeared deceptively docile and harmless. Francois whispered. "Lions function in prides and the ones we see here are most likely just the tip of the iceberg."

He had our full attention as he continued in a serious tone, "The lion is the ultimate killing machine. They are powerful and built for speed. In a charge, they use their muscular body like a battering ram to knock down their prey. A pride can quickly strip an animal's meat off its bones and their rough tongues can literally 'lick the platter clean'. Before long, there is nothing left. Just a bloody spot to mark the place where their victim's death occurred." Francois exchanged a few words with the driver who swerved to get away from the innocent looking cats.

This was no place to have car trouble.

As we pulled away, our white hunter completed his thoughts concerning lions. "In my years of experience, I've learned respect for a lion's speed and their cunning ways. I've found it prudent to just steer clear of them to avert entanglement with these proficient killers." Driving in the dark amongst all the unpredictable predators gave me plenty of anxiety and I was glad when we were safely back to our campsite.

Shortly after our arrival, the main chef, a veteran of the camp for some 30 years, came to greet us. He had the reputation of being the temperamental sort, and rarely, if ever allowed anyone inside his culinary domain. Francois confirmed this by saying, "*Mama*, later in the trip I'll do my best to get you inside his open-air kitchen." Then with tongue in cheek, finished with, "but it may have to be with the aid of my gun."

My shower helped revive me. I headed for the mess tent and sat down in a striped canvas chair to enjoy the ambiance of the crackling fire as I recorded the day's happenings. Inside, Will and Francois were discussing the day's events, so I contented myself by gazing alone at the glowing embers. The heavenly sight overhead defied description and several falling stars caught my attention as they plummeted through the African atmosphere.

My diary kept me occupied while the men plotted and schemed about this and that. I wrote: Tonight, the men are concentrating on four-legged game instead of two-legged dears. Brian and Denny were also in the dining room busily setting up their equipment. It was fascinating to watch them transform the mess tent into a makeshift movie set. Bright lights were clipped onto the tent poles, the camera was seated on its tripod, and Denny was to man the boom mike. During the meal, the camera rolled as Brian interviewed Francois, Will, and me concerning our thoughts on the safari thus far.

Francois spoke first, "One cannot hunt the animals we're seeking by means of the bow, unless one knows the way of its life. The things it loves, it fears, the paths it will follow, the quality of its speed, and the measure of its courage. All these need to be considered."

Will stated, "Over the years, I've noticed that big game animals are smart and seem to know as much about me as I do about them."

Francois agreed, "Yes, and at times they make better use of it." Then with a stern look on his face added, "and when the animal out maneuvers the hunter, the hunter had best be prepared for BIG trouble!"

"Jean, I'm wondering what you think of Africa so far?" Francois queried.

"The Selous is beyond anything I could have imagined. There is an astonishing variety of wildlife here. I consider it a privileged to witness life in this island of security that has been cut out for Africa's amazing animals. The reserve is so secluded from the rest of the world and the animals so special that this place feels sacred to me. Coming on safari has been a journey of discovery about Africa and about myself. I personally would have never chosen to come to such a remote destination, full of wild animals, but I am grateful that I did."

None of us were accustomed to being in the limelight, with the eye of the camera trained on us, but I felt we did okay for amateurs.

I experienced a fretful night's sleep, in anticipation of tomorrows tracking of the wounded buffalo. At dawn, the sound of some local birds announced the new day. Surprisingly, during the night it had cooled off sufficiently so that my blanket felt good. At breakfast, I asked how our server John was doing. I found out that he had been taken to the closest village to have his troublesome tooth extracted and would return as soon as possible.

I could not imagine how primitive their dental procedures were in this bush country. I winced at the thought.

We left camp before the sun had a chance to warm the roofs of our tents. While riding in the open-air vehicles, with the day still young, we wore lightweight jackets to ward off the chilly breezes. The farther we traveled, the more animals we saw. It was exhilarating to view thousands of Cape buffalo, as well as other species of animals, who had been given unusual names like Lichtenstein's Hartebeest, Klipspringers, Nyasaland Wildebeest, and Kudu. We saw a lone female hippo waddling toward her watering hole as wild dogs barked loudly somewhere in the vicinity.

Francois had left a marker on the bank so we could immediately pick up yesterday's trail. We trailed the trackers who had nothing but dark, day-old, dried blood to follow, mile after mile, in the forbidding terrain. The tenacity and thoroughness that our seasoned trackers demonstrated would put Sherlock Holmes to shame. Whenever they lost sight of the blood signs, they would fan out in search of a clue to indicate which direction the animal had traveled. This slow tedious process continued until someone located the needed evidence and then we progressed a bit farther. As we followed the telltale signs over the second ridge, the sun was gaining in intensity. When Will stopped to put on his camo gear to avoid getting sunburned, he remarked, "Finding the bull doesn't look good. The tracking is next to impossible."

While winding our way through the bush, I felt the tension rising from the Frenchman and his trackers. Their anxiety was manifested in their facial expressions and their body language. At one point the situation was so tense, I whispered to Brian, "I'm so naive about the dangers of stalking wounded, wild animals that I don't know enough to be sufficiently scared." Brian smiled and nodded in agreement.

There was an eerie feeling in the air and things seemed unusually quite except for an occasional gust of wind that rustled the corn height grasses we were moving through. After hours of tracking, Will had all but given up hope of ever finding his buffalo.

We rounded a clump of trees and suddenly the leg muscles of our trackers went rigid. The trackers had finally located our black, hairy heap laying stone still in an open field. It is not normal for an animal to be sunning itself in the blistering, hot midday sun so we knew he was dead. We moved in to see our excited archer's prize. Although not a world record, Francois assured Will, "Any rifle hunter would be proud to take this one home." The men's testosterone levels suddenly exploded like fireworks, into a jovial celebration of backslapping and handshaking. Will expressed his profound appreciation for Francois and his tracker's phenomenal skills which had made this moment possible.

Next came the customary picture taking session. I described it this way. The cameraman is tasked with the impossible job of making the animal look three times larger than reality, while at the same time, making the hunter look thinner and younger. After the photographs, Francois supervised his skinners in the ghastly chore of caping the animal for Will's trophy mount and extracting the edible portion for the camp's meat supply. Manyimancu spoke in Swahili to his boss, who in turn, explained to his client, "Manyimancu is Muslim. For him to be able to eat the meat, he asks your permission to make a small incision under the neck to bleed the animal." Will agreed, "but tell him to make the incision where it won't mar the trophy."

Next the men strained and shoved until they turned the heavy, rigor mortised carcass onto its back. Its underside was crawling with a mass of ticks, some as big as the end of my finger. And on top of that, the animal was starting to stink, causing flies to swarm the kill. This sight was too much for me. I quickly removed myself from the most morbid and unpleasant sight I ever hoped to see.

I pressed my back up against a nearby shade tree to record what I had just witnessed. While writing, I overheard Will talking to Francois about me and I strained to hear what was being said. "Yesterday I was worried about Jeannie during the stalk. I motioned Denny to go find her because she had been left alone."

Francois asked, "Well, why didn't he go get her?"

Will continued, "Oh, he misunderstood my hand signals and came directly toward me. That's when I left you and went back, at least 200 yards, to get her before something else did. It is interesting that she was calmly sitting under the tree where Edmond had told her to stay put. She was busy writing and unconcerned that a wounded Cape buffalo was on the loose. This is a good sign that she is going to deal with the hunt better than I expected." Francois said, "I've told Manyimancu that from now on he's to be her protector."

In order to maximize time, Francois relegated some of his men to pick up the jeeps. I was horrified when they loaded both rigs full of animal parts. Next I overheard Will's comments about using the hindquarter and entrails as bait. They did not have to draw me a picture; I could guess from their conversation what was next on the agenda, 'SIMBA'- the undisputed king of beasts!

Once back in camp our safari leader told us to pack up our gear for a trip. He mentioned 'fly camp,' but I did not have the slightest idea what that meant. Francois instructed us, "Hurry with your packing. Under the best of conditions, this trip takes at least four hours, and it is more dangerous traveling at night.

I asked Will, "How many days should I pack for?"

"I have no idea" was his reply. "Pack enough because there's no telling when we'll get back here."

We grabbed a quick bite of lunch, gathered our belongings, and were off on another adventure. Where this place was located, I had no clue. As we forged a trail ever deeper into Africa, I asked Francois what the term 'fly camp' meant. He explained, "It's a term used on safari referring to a temporary advanced camp that is quite a distance from base camp."

I was glad 'fly camp' had nothing to do with tsetse flies!

During our lengthy jeep rides I got a chance to closely observe our safari leader. His demeanor, while dealing with the never-ending details of the safari, made everyone feel confident that things were under control. He never went around with knives, revolvers, or even a watch. There was one thing that never left his side and that was his rifle and the six extra rounds of ammunition he carried on his belt.

With gentle groans and creaks of protest, the jeeps traversed rocky dry riverbeds, dead tree roots, burned out stumps, and clods of hard, dried earth. I asked why all the downed trees? Francois explained, "Those trees are one reason why it's so dangerous traveling in the dark, because any elephant worth his 'peanut' cannot resist the urge to knock one down."

Chapter 10

Luring Lions

Moving farther away from civilization allowed me to gain a greater realization of just how wonderfully unique the Selous Reserve truly was. This obscure animal domain possessed an invigorating energy that I could feel. The workers were thrilled at their chance of a lifetime to take part in a bow hunt. They smiled lightheartedly and laughed as our Land Rovers loaded with supplies, bedding, and food wound their way toward our satellite settlement. Whenever we came to a dried-up stream bed, the jeeps would slowly descend through a labyrinth of brown boulders. Once we reached the bottom, Bakari, our seasoned driver, would skillfully switch gears and with a neck-popping jerk, we would crawl up the opposite embankment at the speed of a heavily laden ant.

Speaking of ants...

We passed numerous amazing ant colonies resembling rust-red tenement houses on another planet. Some were knee-height and others were 20 feet high and 30 to 40 feet in diameter, making them taller and larger than our tents. All were filled with a plethora of crawling critters.

This place was a pest exterminator's gold mine!

Edmond, seeing our astonishment over the gigantic ant dwellings explained, "Those hills are formed from bits of soil mixed with ant saliva."

Wow, building those houses took a lot of ingenuity and spit!

We could not have been more pleased with Will's choice of Francois as our safari leader. Because his good looks would put many movie stars to shame, Will jokingly dubbed him as 'the poor man's Robert Redford.' As we got better acquainted, some of the mystery as to what made this African legend 'tick' became known. He shared,

"When I was young, I loved reading stories about Africa. I was particularly intrigued with its amazing animals. In my late teens, I got a chance to turn my dreams into reality by joining a French paratrooper team heading for African soil. By the ripe old age of 20, I had worked my way up through the ranks and had become a professional hunting guide." He admitted he was unusually young to hold the position. "My clients would stare at me in utter disbelief, at how one so young could produce the game they had come so far to bag. This bush country has gotten in my blood. I am devoted to providing a place of safety for these special animals. I have always been doing this job."

Over the years, Francois had fully developed all the attributes needed to be successful at his trade–the patience of Job coupled with a vast knowledge of animals and tracking. I could sense his enthusiasm for our bow hunt. It gave him a welcome break from the traditional rifle hunts he had led over the past 18 years.

En route to fly camp, night overtook us and suddenly my world became smaller as the trees, rocks, and anthills disappeared into an eerie blackness. Out of nowhere came a …

LOUD BANG!

I jumped! My heart raced!

What was that???

The rough road has caused a blowout," Will said. "You stay in the jeep, and I'll help them with the tire." The tire was quickly changed and as we neared our destination, off in the distance, we heard a shrill elephant scream.

Was it announcing our arrival?

I had no idea what 'fly camp' would be like but surmised that it would not be the Taj Mahal. You could have 'blown me over with a feather' when a Hollywood-like setting came into view. A cozy campfire welcomed us. Underneath a magnificent mango tree was a rectangular table covered in a white linen tablecloth. The 'cherry on top' of this piece of African ambiance were the flickering lanterns that bathed our campsite in a warm, romantic glow.

Unbeknownst to us, Francois had sent workers ahead to set up camp. The men had lashed together stands for our water basins, a shower, and toilet. We even had a small propane refrigerator. I instantly fell in love with this charming location. In my estimation, this place truly felt like heaven on earth. I did not care if we ever went back to Kibaoni. This locale turned out to be our home for the next 19 days.

We later learned that our safari held the distinction of being the first ever to spend nearly the entire hunt in 'fly camp.'

Francois had selected this remote campsite on the edge of the Njenji River, for one reason, and one reason only. It was the stomping grounds of elephant with numerous lions sprinkled in for good measure.

Denny said he was exhausted and went straight to bed. Brian, who was experiencing stomach difficulties, also headed to his tent without eating. He sarcastically attributed his ailment on the fact that his body was going through the pangs of pizza withdrawals. Will asked Rama, the assistant cook, to prepare some of the day's kill for dinner. The cook knew that the buffalo had not been properly aged and tenderized, but since 'the customer is always right' he did his best to please *Big Bwana*. I announced, "All I want is some soup and after dinner, if nobody objects, I'll take my shower."

Sure enough, Will later admitted that the buffalo meat was "as tough as shoe leather."

After bathing, I dressed and sat down at the table to catch up on my note taking. While Will was showering, Francois emerged from his tent dressed in a skimpy white towel. He caught the shocked look on my face and headed straight toward me. In a brazen move, the Frenchman sat down right beside me to wait his turn.

Was this really happening?

As the lanterns flicked my heart fluttered. I tried my best to carry on a coherent conversation. I admit that the sight of this handsome, nearly naked man seated next to me, made it difficult for me to concentrate on his conversation.

Once in bed, I realized that I had just relived my favorite scene from the academy award winning movie *Out of Africa,* when Meryl Streep and Robert Redford had camped out in the bush.

I shall always remember this flirtatious encounter that would send chills down the spine of any red-blooded woman!

The next morning the camp leaders husky voice bellowing out orders to the men, brought wakefulness to those of us who were still sandwiched between the sheets. Before leaving each day, we went through a routine of designated duties. Will did his practice shooting, Brian and Denny checked their film equipment, and I made sure there was emergency food in my backpack and fresh water in everyone's canteens. Francois checked his rifle to make sure it functioned properly, while discussing his plans for the day with the trackers. Edmond and Manyimancu were the only other ones in our party that were allowed to carry rifles. Francois had assigned Manyimancu to protect 'the madam.' He never gave me the slightest inkling that he minded being my '*mama* tender.'

After a hardy breakfast, we left camp with jeeps loaded with the sickening lion bait. Francois was in search of the perfect place to hang the 'meat treat' for the resident felines. Our party had not ventured two miles from camp when we stopped to look at some sizeable '*simba*' tracks. The huge paw prints in the wet sand were undeniable evidence that this section of the Selous was…

Lion Country!

The jeeps followed the trail of massive prints which led to two imposing '*simbas.*' These furious carnivores hold the undisputed distinction of holding the top spot in Africa's food chain. Francois excitedly told Will, "Take the big male and you'll have yourself the world's record with a bow. He weighs 500 pounds!"

Prior to the safari, Will and I had only discussed hunting elephant so I had no clue that he would even consider hunting lions. Now here we were eyeing the magnificent pair who lay half-hidden in the tall weeds along the river's edge. They did not appear to have a care in the world while enjoying La Dulce Vida (the sweet life). The male was no doubt wondering what we were doing in HIS domain?? From his royal lair, he lifted his muscular head to flaunt his impressive thick mane. While his keen eyes intently watched us, his heavy tail never missed a beat stroking the grass.

My eyes were affixed on Francois as he, in turn, surveyed the situation. I could tell from his demeanor that he was formulating a plan of action. Sure enough, after driving a short distance, the Frenchman barked out a few orders in Swahili. We parked and his personnel swung into action. They began combing the riverbank to locate a suitable location to string up the buffalo's hindquarter.

The corps of engineers would have been proud of their impressive accomplishments. Three trees, which were close together, were chosen. The workers began cleared small saplings with their native 'pangas' (machetes) and hatchets. Francois climbed up one of the trees. At the 15-foot level, he commenced lashing their cuttings together. When completed he had fashioned wooden platforms in the branches of two of the largest trees.

Brian set up his tripod to film the lengthy building project. Since this ambitious undertaking was an all-day affair, Will took advantage of his down time to sharpen his broadheads, anticipating the action that was sure to come his way. We used this opportunity to talk amongst ourselves as he tested the razor sharp broadheads by trimming the hairs off the back of his arms.

"I sure hope the kids are doing okay," I said. Will remarked while reaching into his tool bag, "They'd really get a kick out of seeing all the animals." I thought about it for a minute then said, "I'm actually glad they're not around the wild animals because I'd hate to lose them out here. You know how Jared always wanders off exploring something that intrigues him, and we panic until he's found." Will laughed. "You're right. It would be impossible to fence off a play area out here. The animals would think we were using them as live bait."

I didn't even want to think about this gruesome scenario.

About that time, Francois called down to me from up in the tree blind. "*Mama*, I need more lashing rope and an ax. Will you please go back to camp and get them for me?"

I was thrilled to be asked to help. I took Manyimancu and Tovano, a jeep driver, with me. We headed toward 'fly camp' by way of the *mkondo*. The soil in this creek had been deeply cut by water during the rainy season, making the sides very steep. Tovano had to shift into first gear in order to descend, and then shift again, as he crossed the stream bed to gain enough speed to climb up the opposite embankment. Unfortunately, his timing technique was off, and the jeep stalled repeatedly while attempting to climb out of the creek. Tovano had no choice but to leave us in the jeep and walk to get help.

This left Manyimancu and me alone, in the jeep, for quite a while. He would smile. I smiled back. Then we sat in silence. I pointed to something. He looked at it and acknowledged with a nod. Then we again experienced an unpleasant silence.

It was very frustrating not being able to communicate. He knew no English. Why should he, this was his country. At this point in the safari, I had picked up several Swahili words.

Francois had taught me the words for hot water but saying '*magi ya moto*' was not applicable in this situation. '*Acha*' meant stop, but we were already at a standstill. '*Twende*' meant let's go, '*Polo Pole*' was slow, and '*Haraka*' meant let's go. Francois said these words all the time but saying them now would sound ridiculous.

I searched around in my bag for something to eat. "Want roll" I said in baby talk as I held it out for him. Manyimancu answered. '*Tafadhali*,' Oh, I remembered that meant please.

We communicated!

And then he said *Asante*, Swahili for thank you. We smiled at each other as we ate. He began speaking in Swahili. I listened intently and picked out a word or two. *Tembo* meant elephant. *Bwana* meant Will. *Mama*, that was me. Manyimancu then pantomimed pulling an *upinde*. I supposed that meant bow. I also recognized *mshale* which meant arrow. This was truly an exercise in human relations.

A more experienced driver finally rescued us. We got the items Francois needed and hurried back to the construction site. Since all the workers were busy chopping down trees for the blind, Francois called down asking me to help feed Brian, Denny, and Will their lunch. I located the basket, spread out the picnic cloth, opened the coolers, and began serving. The cooks had packed rolls, canned meat and tuna fish, fresh fruit, boiled eggs, and boiled white potatoes. We decided that the most appealing dish was rice and bean concoction. We eagerly consumed our tasty lunch. When we had finished, I went over to the base of the tree, where Francois was lashing the flooring together. "Are you and the workers ready to eat?" He indicated that they would stop for lunch.

He called down, "*Mama*, please bring over the rice and beans for the blacks." My face went red with embarrassment, as I confessed that we had unknowingly eaten their food.

Luckily, they did not string me up for lion bait.

After lunch, Will and Francois decided it would be best if they stayed in the tallest tree blind. Brian and Denny were relegated to the smaller shorter blind. Between now and bedtime, they had to figure out how to get themselves and their camera, sound gear, spare parts, and tools into their cramped sleeping quarters.

The camera was rolling as we watched one of the jeeps hoist up the buffalo's heavy hindquarter into a third tree near the other blinds. Denny had Zuberi climb up and tape a microphone on a limb directly over the lion's *piece de resistance,* which dangled enticingly from the end of a hefty rope. Denny could now record every thrilling moment. The building project was complete once leafy branches were added as camouflage to the 'high-rise' sleeping quarters. Will crawled up in his blind and made several test shots to help him ascertain the distance and angles needed to reach the bait.

In lieu of the spotlights customarily used to announce the grand opening of a newly opened establishment, the jeeps dragged some buffalo intestines down the sandy river bottom, in front of the lion's noses before circling back towards the bait. Tonight's chef's special was aged buffalo butt. This unorthodox marketing plan stimulated the hungry lions sufficiently that, in broad daylight, they followed the trail of tripe to the bait.

The eight-hour herculean task was now complete, and we drove back to camp against a kaleidoscopic sunset. These spectacular fiery skies always stimulated Brian's creative juices. Once he put the camera right on the ground and focused on a jeep tire as it drove through a puddle of water. After following the ripples, he slowly panned skyward towards the sunset. Another time, I was near my tent brushing my hair and Brian filmed me in silhouette against a bright red sky. Brian would later intersperse these artistic touches into our documentary.

Back at camp, the men freshened up, grabbed some take-along food, and loaded their mattresses, pillows, and blankets into the jeeps. Before he left, Will verbally recorded this entry about the day's happenings. "We spotted a lion and lioness-a nice big lion with a good mane. Francois fashioned two blinds on the banks nearby. The buffalo's hindquarters were strung up in an adjacent tree. I needed to practice for when the lions came to the bait, so I climbed up the tree. My shoots towards the buffalo rump, at 15 yards, were good. I also hit the target at 30 yards. This project took all day. It looks like we are going to spend the night up in the blind, on a mattress, waiting for the lions to come feed at daybreak. It is Tuesday evening, September 23, 1986, and I am tired."

I, of course, remained behind in camp to let the men have their night of terror all to themselves. I spent my free time writing as fast as I could to catch up on the day's activities. When the men showed up in camp the next morning, I thought for sure they would have gotten the lion. Instead, the jeeps drove up. The tired, dejected men piled out, and nobody uttered a word.

Being an intuitive individual, I could tell they had not succeeded in reaching their goal.

During breakfast Francois explained what had happened. "The cats came to the bait, but they sensed that something wasn't quite right. Consequently, they were reluctant to eat the bait." Will followed up with more details. "The lions sniffed and growled around our trees a good portion of the night." Denny interjected this detail. "To be exact, they spent four hours underneath the blinds. At daybreak, the cats laid down nearby, but sadly not within bow range." Between bites of breakfast, Edmond shed further light on the subject. "The time of day that the lions are in bow range is imperative because no game can be taken in the Selous after dark. Spotlighting of animals is, of course, a 'no-no,' and the females and young of all species are always protected."

Denny and Brian kept us in stitches as they recounted their sleepless night of incredible discomfort in their blind. Brian's large frame faced the bait with the camera between his already cramped legs. Denny said, "I faced the opposite direction and straddled the sound gear with Brian's stinky feet right in my face." Brian retorted, "Oh yeah, your feet didn't smell like rosebuds either." Brian described that changing positions, for comfort sake, was a major ordeal because movement had to be done simultaneously and noiselessly.

Denny spent the entire night listening with his headphones, as the lions warily surveyed their new open-air eating establishment. He had forgotten that when the recorder reached the end of a tape it automatically shut off. "About 2 a.m. the tape machine suddenly clicked off and all noises in the vicinity ceased. The silence was deafening. It was broken when the lions, prowling around nearby, came right underneath our tree and started sniffing around." The frightened men openly admitted that, at that point, they were afraid to breathe. We got a good laugh out of listening to their first experience in a lion blind.

Francois suggested that we should wait a few days to return to the bait site. "This will give the lions a chance to feel more at ease and give the human scent, especially Brian's foot odor, time to clear out." This comic relief caused us to almost fall out of their chairs laughing.

Chasin' Elephant

Edmond said, "Today we hope to get a hippopotamus to use as bait, because it is one of the lions favorites. We will find some wallowing in a nearby water hole." The fact that lions can eat through the thick rubbery hide of a hippo made me realize just how sharp their teeth are. But instead of pursuing hippos, we got distracted by a lone bull elephant feasting in some nearby trees.

Spotting an elephant is a learned art. Big as they are they are seldom conspicuous, since their coloring helps them blend in with the environment. t was equally astonishing that such a large, heavy creature could slip so quietly through the brush. Mile after mile, our safari party pursued the colossus. When he stopped to eat, Francois skillfully maneuvered Will into position for a shot within 25 paces of the jungle patriarch.

Will stepped out from the cover of his tree and shot. Sadly, his arrow missed the hoped-for heart shot. Once struck, the bull took off at a remarkably fast clip. Although their normal walking speed is 4 to 5 miles per hour, they can run, for short distances, as fast as 25 miles per hour. Will's shot had caused this grey giant to shift into 'high gear.' To keep pace with the fast-moving mammal, we could not stop for even a second. I struggled to keep up with the men's longer strides. For every step they took, my shorter legs made two or three additional ones. I was not used to this pace. After a while, each step became more painful than the last. My hands, wet with perspiration, had to continuously push aside the many low hanging branches destined to slap me in the face. My bare legs and arms took a beating from sharp thorns as I scurried by. I stumbled, recovered, and ran on so as not to be left behind. After several hours of running and fast-paced walking, the trackers stopped.

The trackers had located the bull in a grove of trees, foraging for food, with two other tuskers. Will was in the process of making his stalk, when suddenly the area was alive with what resembled a pachyderm picnic. Six cows and several youngsters showed up in the shady haven to lunch with the bulls. They were likely lured there by the abundant low hanging branches-just the right height for shorter trunks. The game scouts referred to the young bulls as 'mommy's boys' because they remain with their mothers for years. The teenaged bulls began plowing up the turf with their tusks. Once their favorite bulbs were unearthed, their social protocol dictated that they would willingly share the taste treat with other family members.

Francois' body language spoke volumes as to when we were in a dangerous predicament. If he felt we were safe he carried his .460 up on his shoulder, but if he suspected trouble, he held the powerful firearm in front of him as he walked. A quick look in his direction confirmed my suspicions about the seriousness of our situation. He had a death grip on his rifle! His face was another gauge of our degree of danger. The Frenchman's facial Richter scale was currently registering this silent warning:

It does not get more dangerous than this...Don't Anybody Move!

I later learned that there is not a more aggressive animal in the world than female elephants who are protecting their young. In fact, the cow elephants use a group effort to keep their youth safe from harm. The more experienced matriarchs are designated as 'nursery leaders' that oversee their vulnerable young. Unlike their Asian counterparts, African cows are equipped with tusks. At birth, their offspring are already three feet tall, covered with hair, and weigh a whopping 200 pounds. By nine months, the calves tip the scales around 750 pounds making them a force to be reckoned with.

While waiting for the females and their 'kiddos' to move on, we remained frozen in place with the full fury of the afternoon sun beating down on us. The heat was exacerbated by the pain we were experiencing from standing in one position for an extended period. I needed a distraction to help take my mind off the misery my body was experiencing.

I began focusing my attention on the big bulls. Since we were down wind, the lunching elephants were unaware of our presence. The magnificent mammals moved peacefully through their habitat with inconceivable gentleness. Occasionally they stopped to break off edible leaves and tender shoots with their trunks. I enjoyed this rare opportunity to observe the quadrupeds blissfully going about their daily lives.

I began thinking about the attributes of the Black workers assigned to our safari. They were polite and compassionate toward me. When trudging through the bush, they would occasionally carry my backpack. They would also point out sharp thorns to avoid and even held back foliage destined to hurt me. It was surprising how much of the flora in Africa had thorns. Edmond once remarked, "If you get hung up on one of those long thorns, you will have no choice, but to wait to dislodge yourself from those aptly named 'wait-a-bit' trees." During a calmer period in the safari, I stuck one of those long thorns into a tree truck. It easily penetrated the wood and came out unscathed.

The workers, except Edmond, wore black rubber sandals. Their feet were totally exposed to the elements except for two crisscross straps which held the shoe in place. Through the years, the skin on their feet had become toughened and, at times while tracking the natives preferred to go barefoot. To those of us who grew up wearing shoes to protect our feet it was unbelievable. This incongruous scenario reminded me of one of Will's sarcastic sayings, "When it's too tough for everyone else-it's just right for us."

Suddenly, one of the young bulls started ambling in our direction. My boredom now turned to terror as the mountain-sized object moved dangerously close to where we were standing. It appeared that this was not yet an aggressive advance. This hungry teenager was probably just looking for more food to fill his 'hollow leg.' While gazing in our direction, he just stood there swinging his trunk from side to side, deciding, should I stay, or should I go? One wrong move on our part and it would be all over. Had he ascertained that humans where close by, he would have alerted the others who would have made mincemeat out of us. We all breathed easier when he moved off in another direction. Luckily, we had once again averted a potential disaster.

While we were unable to move, the big bull we were after, 'out foxed' us by going elsewhere. Due to the profusion of fresh footprints, each about 2 feet in diameter, the trackers were unable to determine which print belonged to our elephant. So, after all our effort and energy expended, 'Big Grey' got away. The famous French saying *C'est la vie*– 'Such is Life,' was certainly applicable to this frustrating turn of events.

Will and I had no way of calculating how many miles we had walked and run that day, but we guessed about 10. And on top of that we were starving. Chasing an aggravated elephant, 'hot footing' it though the bush had left no time for a lunch break. Not only were we exhausted, famished, and frustrated at losing the elephant, but we were also a considerable distance from our transportation. Contemplating our recent brush with death, I was simply glad to be alive and hungry. I suddenly recalled that my backpack held the solution to my being able to get back to the jeeps without being dragged or carried. I found a packet of energy powder and mixed it in my collapsible cup with some water from the canteen. This gave me the needed 'oomph' to get myself back to our rigs. I sat my hot, weary body down to recover from our day's long ordeal. I could now empathize with new Army recruits while, at boot camp, when their drill sergeant has worked them to within an inch of their lives.

Brian and Denny were feeling especially exhausted since the night before they had experienced a sleepless night in the blind. The two men likened chasing elephant all day, without food or rest, to having participated in the infamous World War II Bataan Death March imposed on U.S. prisoners by the Imperial Japanese army.

Out of the corner of my eye, I noticed something unbelievable.

My tired mind must have been playing tricks on me - NO, it really was the flicker of fire. Francois and Edmond had turned into pyromaniacs! Yes, there they were lighters in hand setting the tall dry grasses on fire. We were aghast at this shocking happening. It was like watching someone setting fire to an animal shelter. The bush veterans detected our shock and intense disapproval. I could not conceive of why they would do such a thing.

Francois, noting how peeved I was, patiently explained, "Burning is an integral part of the wildlife conservation practices we use during the dry season." Edmond also shed some light on the subject. "The grazing animals simply cannot consume all the grass. The excess dies off and, if not burned within two or three years, it becomes thick and matted which suppresses the growth of new shoots. So timely burning removes old grass, promotes fresh growth, which also prevents soil erosion that takes place whenever grass dies. Burning also suppresses the growth of woody plants. If left unchecked they create dense thickets and reduce the extent of grasslands available to grazing animals.

Human settlements make the seasonal migration patterns of large game impossible, so animals are encouraged to move within the reserve and fire is a convenient method of achieving that. The animals enjoy the flush of fresh green grasses that follow a fire."

I wanted to know what happens to the animals during a fire. Francois fielded my inquiry. "Most of the larger species instinctively seek shelter or simply move out of the way of the flames. Some smaller creatures, like mice or snakes are killed, but most escape by crawling under boulders and others shelter down inside burrows. Insects probably suffer the most. Birds, of course, fly away unless an accidental fire takes place late in the season after nesting has begun, but this is highly unusual." Edmond added, "Fire, selective culling, and the fact that humans don't live in the Selous, are reasons why the game population is many times greater than it was when the first Europeans came into Tanzania." I said, "I'm sure glad you explained the positive aspects of burning. I feel better about what you just did." This reserve truly is an island in a sea of humanity.

Francois possessed a sixth sense about what would make life more pleasant for his guests. Unbeknownst to us, before leaving camp, he had given instructions to his personnel to spruce up things in and around our campsite. A grass partition had been erected between the dining and the domestic work area. At one end of the divider, they formed a charming arch as a passageway. The shower and toilet had also been made more private, which pleased me the lone woman in camp. The outdoor toilet was now at least 300 feet (the length of a football field) away from our campsite. For me, this distance was a two-edged sword, great from a privacy standpoint, but downright frightening after dark. I dreaded 'the trip out back' because of the animals that roamed at night. Will graciously escorted me to the outhouse on the few nights he was not sleeping in the tree blind. The other nights, I just prayed for an early dawn.

Waterbuck's Waterloo

We will all remember September 25, as a day of near catastrophe. It started around 4 a.m. when Will decided to tinker with his archery equipment. Because he was hunting practically around the clock, he said he felt like he was 'behind the power curve,' so he got up early to make sure his bow equipment was functioning properly.

About 6 a.m., Will's declaration, "I've done something stupid," resounded against our tent walls. I sat straight up in bed and was shocked by what he was showing me in the beam of his flashlight. A blood-soaked handkerchief wrapped tightly around his left hand!

I blurted out, "What on earth happened to your hand?"

He sheepishly explained, "I was checking the elephant broadheads for durability when one suddenly broke under test pressure causing the arrow to recoil. The freshly sharpened razor blade struck my hand tearing a gash between my thumb and index finger. That's the exact place where the bow handle fits my hand."

"Oh no, we'd better get Francois over here quick."

Once appraised of his client's injury, Francois grabbed his medical bag and came to the rescue. Our bush doctor rose to the challenge by adroitly tending to Will's urgent need and bandaging his hand. I watched in utter disbelief as they camouflaged the white medical tape with camo spray paint and got ready for the day. For a less determined soul this accident would have ended our safari, but undaunted Will left on the hunt although his hand was hurting badly.

As we drove along, the bow adventurer's streak of bad luck continued. Will noticed something amiss with one of his bows and reached into his tool bag to retrieve a gadget to tighten the loosened part. In his zeal to repair it, he applied too much pressure causing it to fly into pieces. One of the fragments struck me in the corner of my right eye. Fortunately, all I received was a small scratch. We collectively agreed, "We're afraid to be near you today; you're jinxed."

On our drive we spotted numerous animals. Some of them made outlandish sounds as we approached. The hartebeest emitted a nasal puffing snort. The zebras yapped and whined like dogs. The impalas leapt an unbelievable 30 feet in each long graceful bound to keep a comfortable distance from our jeeps. Our safari expert informed us, "These amazing antelope are only as tall as a goat, but they can run as fast as 50 miles per hour." I was particularly enamored with this beautiful antelope because its golden-brown color contrasted with a white underbelly making it appear as delicate as it was graceful.

At midday, we had lunch underneath several shade trees. Will, Francois, Denny, and Brian took a short nap afterwards because in several hours they would be spending another sleepless night in the blind. The remainder of the afternoon was spent trying to find Will an elephant, but nothing materialized. Just before dark the men climbed their respective tree houses. I returned to camp, where before retiring, I enjoyed a delicious meal and relaxing conversation with Edmond.

The next morning, I heard the disappointing details of how the lions had again evaded the tree-top dwellers. "The cats stayed around eating all night long" Will said, "but at daybreak they went elsewhere to pick their teeth."

We left camp hoping for some good luck to come our way. As we motored along the Njenji riverbed, Francois spotted two waterbucks involved in an intense argument. The jeeps came to a standstill. Without the breeze from the jeep's movement, the heat was stifling. We watched the males embroiled in a territorial feud. Francois spoke softly in Swahili to the driver, *'polo pole'*, take it easy. The bucks had squared off and were involved in a furious life or death struggle. Consequently, they were unaware of our approaching vehicles. Brian readied his camera. His hands were less hot from the sun than from the excited pounding in his chest, sensing he was witnessing a remarkable filming opportunity.

Will grabbed his 90-pound compound bow, carefully aimed, and made a shot at the unbelievable distance of 67 yards. His arrow soared gracefully through the air before penetrating completely through the mid-section of the largest preoccupied male, who never knew what hit him. After a few frantic bounds, the lethal broadhead brought him down. We jumped out of the jeeps and ran toward the fallen buck. We found him *kufa,* dead in his weed covered battle ground. As we approached, we noticed his infuriated opponent still ramming the dead animal with his sharp horns to emphasize the fact that he was victorious. To our amazement, we had to run his competitor off.

Francois measured the buck's horns as Will anxiously awaited the results. "A respectable twenty-six and a quarter inches." Will asked, "Is that going to place?" Francois confidently assured Will, "It will be near the top of the world record for bow. The men are impressed with your archery skills. In their estimation '*Bwana* Roberts' is their hero."

"Gee, that's a beautiful animal," I said. The hefty antelope's body was shades of grey, brown, which darkened to black at its long, slender face. The striated horns curved as they extended upwards into sharp points.

Following the caping of the animal, a portion of the waterbuck's hindquarter was destined for the lion's meat market. The buffalo meat was now spoiled to the point that it would 'gag a maggot.' Now even hungry lions would not touch it. Back in camp, the edible portion of the waterbuck was hung up to age on a tree in the kitchen. After it was properly aged, the cooks would tenderize it with their meat mallets to make it edible.

The following day, we left camp in hopes of finding a bull elephant. Francois mentioned, "One of the keys to locating them, especially for bow hunters, is finding them in and around their water sources where they drink and bathe daily. Otherwise, in these bone-dry conditions, they stay hidden in the dense brush. There you can't see them until you're practically on top of them, maybe 18 to 20 yards away." Francois continued educating us about elephants. "They are very resourceful. In the grip of this dry season, when water is scarce, they utilize their tusks to drill holes into the sandy river bottoms, about two to three inches underneath the surface. To extract the life-giving liquid, they insert their trunks into the holes. In a miraculous way the sand is filtered out as they drink."

Now I know what had caused the numerous holes I had noticed in the river bottoms.

Francois continued, "Elephants also use their tusks to forage for food. They plough up the ground to locate delectable roots and they also pry tree branches apart to get at the soft moist cores. When necessary these tusks become lethal weapons. The monetary worth of these immense ivory teeth makes them particularly vulnerable to money-hungry poachers, who could care less what age or sex an elephant may be."

Our hopes of finding an elephant withered as we walked for miles in the merciless sun, which showed us not one ounce of mercy. Our misery was intensified by the fact that we saw not a single animal to help take our minds off the hellish heat. This was the hottest day of the entire trip, and we gladly took refuge underneath a large leafy tree. We collapsed in a puddle of sweat in its shade to get some welcome relief from the relentless rays, as we ate a snack from my emergency provisions.

I wanted to learn about Francois' favorite animal, the elephant. His stories confirmed what we had previously observed that cows are wonderful mothers. He recollected, "I have witnessed Earth's most fascinating mothers doing some remarkable things. Once I watched a female lifting her youngster up on her enormous tusks in order to carry it across the raging Nile River. Another time I observed four cows, during a rainstorm, standing in a circle with their foreheads touching. Their ears were spread open like giant, grey umbrellas. Underneath their babies were napping dry and contented. I marvel at their intelligence and their protectiveness." "That's fantastic," I said. "Protection and concern for one another are worthy traits in man and beast."

I have noticed that their ears seem to be an indicator of their mood. Is my observation correct?" Edmond agreed. "Speaking of ears, elephants have the largest in the world. Each sail-like appendage weighs a whopping 110 pounds! Elephants are endowed with keen hearing, which compensates for their extremely small eyes. They use their ears as a built-in cooling system to help regulate their body temperature. By flapping them like fans, air is forced over a network of blood vessels close to the surface, which in turn cools their blood."

We all agreed that no sane elephant would be out in this stifling heat and that we had experienced enough of the sun's vengeance for one day. We got in our jeeps just in time to see a lone jackal up ahead on the river bottom. We inched our way toward him. He caught sight of us but did not seem inclined to run. This was highly unusual since most of the animals we encountered were very wary of humans and made every effort to shun contact with us. Francois whispered to the driver *twende*, let's get going.

Our driver 'put the peddle to the metal' and we went flying across the sandy river bottom beside the now sprinting jackal, much like Indians galloping alongside their enemy's in an action-packed Western movie. The frightened jackal soon made its way up the bank and disappeared out of sight. I hate to admit it, but I quite enjoyed our exhilarating jackal chase.

Tanzanian women

Trip to main camp

Antelopes at M'barangandu River

Will shooting bow

Jean, Will, Denny, and Francois picknicking

Camera crew records men's plans

Cape Buffalos

Francois our expedition leader

Long-needled thorns

Females protecting their young

Satellite camp beneath mango tree

Cooking on banks of Rufuji River

Jean samples
worker's food

River water
collected for use
in fly camp

Francois building
tree blinds

Francois, Jean, and Will spend night in
blind

Lion and lioness near blind

Will drinking from a puddle

Bull elephants in bush

Jean climbs tree amidst sausages

Giant ant hills

Bait meat hanging near blind

Trackers: Rembe, Kisenga
(hat), and Zuberi

Jean visits with Francois
and his tracker

Porter carries bow case on head

Jean outside tent at sundown

Successfull expedition group photo

Chapter 13

Rude Awakening

Common sense dictated that Denny get a good night's sleep because he was not feeling up to par. He had awakened the previous day with a troublesome earache, and to add insult to injury, a cold sore had blossomed on his lower lip. In retrospect, it was a blessing that Denny stayed in camp with me while Will, Francois, and Brian were holed up in their tree top abodes.

Before retiring I made some much-needed journal entries, watched the dying embers of the campfire fade, and headed for my canvas quarters. I tended to my sole housekeeping duty, which consisted of moving our clean clothing from our rubber mattresses on the floor, into our river bags. The fantastic service we were receiving was a welcome break from my morn till night hectic schedule back home.

I was tired, so sleep came easily. About 1 a.m. I was jolted awake by a severe pain in my left hip, just below the waist. It felt as if I had been stabbed with a knife blade. As consciousness became a reality, I felt a multi-legged intruder moving inside my nightgown! Because of its many legs, I surmised I had been stung by a scorpion. I determined that quick action was necessary before it nabbed me again.

Sitting upright, I grabbed the material of my nightgown where the movement was occurring and squeezed with all my might. As I released the flimsy fabric, I heard the faint sound of something falling onto the sheets. My hands were shaking as I groped around in the dark for my flashlight. I located it and pressed the on switch. I saw a squished scorpion. I deduced that, at best, its poison would cause me pain and perhaps make me sick; then a scary thought crossed my mind.

Would it kill me?

Unzipping the tent, I ran outside and let out a despairing cry for Denny's help. My heart was pounding, and it seemed to be keeping pace with the tent door flapping in the breeze. The pain was getting worse as I impatiently waited for Denny's arrival.

In my state of panic, I thought, where's Will when I need him? Oh yes, he's up in some stupid tree probably snoring his head off.

When Denny saw the dead scorpion, he tried to reassure me by saying, "Jean, I'm almost certain this variety of scorpion isn't the deadly sort."

I hoped that with a master's degree in wildlife ecology, he knew what he was talking about. But since my life could possibly be at risk, I asked if he would show it to Edmond. Denny left with the remains of the lifeless creature in its tissue coffin. While waiting for my 'second opinion' I started feeling sick to my stomach. My mind was considerably eased when Denny came back with Edmond's reassuring report, "This '*nge,*' scorpion, is young, so your pain will feel like a severe bee sting and last for about 24 hours." This was the good news that I was hoping for.

Denny and I were curious to see what else might be lurking in my tent. Our search unearthed one additional small scorpion in the corner near the foot of my mattress. Denny gave me some aspirin, then went to check his tent for '*nges.*' He too zealously evicted a couple from his quarters.

After my unnerving incident, I was not able to immediately get back to sleep. Eventually, the medicine took effect, and a feeling of drowsiness came over me. On the wings of sleep my beleaguered body was carried beyond the realm of things that go 'ouch' in the night.

Shortly after daybreak, the men returned from their 'limb lodgings' dead-tired, discouraged, and empty handed. The lions had come for their nightly meal but had denied Will even a sneak peek during daylight hours. When Francois heard that a scorpion had stung me, he immediately dispatched a driver to main camp with instructions to bring back cots for Mama and the others.

Next, he told Japhet, "Take everything out of '*Mama's*' tent and give it a thorough house cleaning. When you are finished, replace her mattress with my cot until her bed arrives. '*Mama*,' please excuse us while we conduct a 'search and destroy mission' in your tent for free loaders who are not paying their rent." Sure enough, Japhet found one additional scorpion in my tent. While he went to get Francois' bed, I placed masking tape over the many torn places in the canvas fabric. When I finished, the tent's patch job resembled a decorated purple heart veteran returning from war. In all, they found and destroyed seven scorpions in and around our sleeping quarters. Francois referred to them as babies. The fully grown ones he said are seven or more inches long. "Apparently," he teased, "they're using her tent as a nursery for their young."

Francois also confirmed that I would be okay by saying "Of the more than 1,000 species of scorpions, only one type (bark scorpions) has a sting that can kill people."

I was glad, with experiences like this that I was unfamiliar with life in the African bush. That way I did not have to worry, in advance, about what might happen and could concentrate instead on what was happening at that moment.

With the trauma of the scorpions over, we were hungry and ready to eat breakfast. Francois knew just what I needed to take my mind off my misery. I sat entranced listening to another one of his astounding experiences. "I once guided a *Punjab* from India, who had come to hunt leopard. He brought with him an entourage of servants including an armed guard to protect his precious jewels. He would majestically enter the mess tent, and his servants would seat the gigantic man at a private table apart from the rest. Then they would bring out his jewel box and drape him with an ornate necklace which contained a jeweled insignia of his high office. His servants helped prepare all his meals. They were served on the dishes they had brought from India. No one else was in his social class so he dined all alone and drank gin...LOTS of it, far into the night. Then the servants would lead their very lonely, inebriated excellency to his quarters."

How sad I thought, all that 'poor' rich man needed was someone to love and befriend him.

Night of Terror

The safari personnel stayed busy on reconnaissance missions between our Njenji fly camp and Kibaoni. Their errands included taking Brian's camera batteries to be charged on the main camp's generator, sending and delivering messages, taking out the garbage, delivering food, and now bringing beds.

Will suggested that we use Sunday as a day of rest to give our nerves, bodies, and spirits a breather. Will fine-tuned his archery equipment. Brian wrote letters home. "Many of my photo shoots keep me away from Provo, for long periods of time. I wish it weren't that way, but it is."

I was tired of wearing khaki colored clothing. I changed into a striped T-shirt and a pair of Bermuda shorts and used my manicure kit to make my roughened hands more presentable.

While we rested, Francois took Denny and some workers to check on a piece of buffalo meat that had been placed up on a tree limb to attract a black leopard. Because the lions were acting unusually persnickety, Francois surprised us by building a new blind at another location. He hoped that a change of scenery might make the wary animals feel more relaxed so they would stay around during daylight hours. This time he constructed one big platform, in a sausage tree, and hung the bait from a nearby tree. The film crew's blind was eliminated to cut down on the noise and human scent. Late in the day, Francois returned to camp. He had noticed a sickly-looking Cape buffalo. "If we don't take it, the lions surely will. After all our hard work, I don't want the cat's attention diverted to a live kill."

The trackers were able to put Will right on to the ailing buffalo. After an easy stalk, he made a successful shot. It was added to the lion's meat market in hopes that the fresh supply would be so tempting that they could not resist an all-you-can-eat feast.

We drove by some Marabou storks wading is some shallow pools. Brian signaled for us to stop. He get some footage of the majestic birds then he suddenly leapt out of his jeep and started running across the sand. At first, it seemed as if he had gone mad, however, his intent was to get the birds to fly away so he could capture their enormous wing spans. It was a spectacular sight.

While picking up the men's bedding, Francois posed a seemingly preposterous question to me. "*Mama*, will you join us tonight in the new enlarged hideaway? You will never experience this type of thrill at Disney's Adventure Land." All heads turned in my direction awaiting my answer. I heard my voice nonchalantly responding, "I'll give it a try." Few would have put their money down on my accepting his mind-blowing offer. Little did they know that I would consider this as my chance of a lifetime. Opportunity was knocking, notwithstanding the fact that hungry lions were a mere 15 feet below! *Before ascending the tree, I had a good talk with my bladder that it must hold out until morning. The men had their emergency 'pee can,' but there was no way that I could hit that small object, in the dark, with three men inches away.*

With a great deal of trepidation, I headed up the tree, amongst the long sausages dangling from its branches. Whenever my five-foot frame found it impossible to reach the next limb, I used Will's leg as a step stool to get where I needed to be. With considerable help and encouragement from the men, I reached the blind. My resting place was between Francois and Will. After the frightful assent I was panting and feeling shaky, but gradually I regained my composure. I was no 'Tom Boy' and had never climbed a tree, so it was not as easy as 'Tarzan and Jane' made it look in the movies.

The blind's amenities consisted of one old lumpy mattress. This was not the Ritz, but better than the board bed at the beach hotel.

After eating our meager meal in silence, I turned my attention to a fascinating panorama of red hues emerging in the western sky. I used this time to make some journal entries. One notation contained thoughts that I had never shared with anyone. It was my reasoning for being open to the invitation to stay in the blind. Years earlier, I had mentally pictured a bedroom with a retractable roof. When opened it revealed a glass ceiling which allowed my love and I to lay in bed and gaze at the sky above. By taking advantage of this opportunity, my dream of watching the stars in bed had come true!

My original plans did not include lions roaming around underneath.

As the blanket of darkness came over us, I laid back to soak up all the sights and sounds that the evening had to offer. The night sky was clear, allowing moonbeams to stream in on us through the leafy branches being used as camouflage. I lay immersed in a labyrinth of shimmering leaves. I embraced these magical moments to fill my whole being. I watched in awe as countless stars began spreading their celestial glory in an amazing array of astrological patterns. These sights were the most magnificent that I had ever witnessed since there were no electric lights for miles to bar their brilliance.

When the wind changed direction, the clear air was now filled with a putrid odor. Will described the smell when he whispered, "It's like spending the night at a garbage dump." It also brought with it a new awareness. I became cognizant of the incessant noise of buzzing flies swarming the rotting meat.

I was enjoying my exceptional experience in the leafy treetops, so much so, that I had almost forgotten why we were there. I was jolted back into reality when Francois, who was reclining on the mattress next to me, suddenly sat straight up. He cocked his keen ears and scarcely seemed to breathe. I strained to hear what had gotten his attention. Soon, I too heard the crackling sounds of something walking through the dried leaves beneath our tree. When he noticed the alarm on my face, Francois leaned my way and whispered, "It's just some hyena prowling about. They won't stay around long because they're afraid of the lions."

They weren't the only ones scared of them!

Suddenly the intimidating roar of a lion sent shivers up and down my spine. This imposing sound had the intended effect of striking terror into the hearts of every man and beast within the reach of its horrific voice. Oddly, it seemed to be coming from the direction of our camp.

When the Land-Rovers came to retrieve us the next day, we had not seen 'hide nor hair' of the lion. Back at camp, Denny and Edmond had everyone's undivided attention as they unfolded the astounding story of their incredible night of terror. Earlier in the evening our sound specialist and Manyimancu had taken a ride to view animals. After dinner, Denny was able to record the natives singing their traditional Maasai songs and chants, which are so much a part of Africa.

Once everyone retired, the moon's rays, on the embankment behind our encampment, captured the shadows of two large creatures sneaking into the kitchen. It was none other than Will's huge lion and lioness lured there by our meat supply.

Denny's eyes began to widen as he unfolded the horrifying details of his encounter with the lions. "I was awakened out of a sound sleep, by prowlers violently shaking and clawing at our meat supply hanging in the kitchen. It fell down with a loud thud right next to my tent. Then came jaws ripping apart the skin and bones." The hairs on the back of my neck stood straight up as he continued recounting his dealings with the brazen lions. Denny admitted, "I lay frozen with fear under the psychological protection of my flimsy bed covers, praying that the felines were not in the mood for dessert at my expense!"

Edmond piped in, "I heard the commotion and grabbed my gun." He continued relating how he left his tent to see if shining his *'torch'* into the kitchen would scare off the midnight marauders. He recognized the two lions as the ones who were supposed to be at the REAL bait sight. He had a two-fold purpose in trying to run the lions off. One was, of course, for safety and he also did not want to get into a situation where he had to shoot, because our hunting party only had one lion permit. No matter who took the lion, it would count as Will's kill.

Edmond, had us mesmerized as he continued, "Only the female was frightened away by my torch. The massive mound of masculinity just lay there, his eyes glowing more intently as my light moved in his direction. He was not intimidated by a human pointing a beam of light at him. The uninvited diner's eyes defiantly leered back at me while devouring his midnight snack. I could do nothing short of shooting him, so I crept back inside my tent and nervously waited for him to finish up and be on his way."

Francois had a serious look on his face, as he shared a personal experience concerning lions coming into camp. "A lion can cut a man in half with one slap of his powerful paw. I know, because recently a lioness dragged one of my fellow white hunters from his tent in the night, mauled, and killed him!!"

Up until now, I had assumed: I was safe in camp. Well, as a popular song from Gershwin's opera Porgy and Bes says - "It ain't necessarily so."

From numerous conversations with Will, prior to the hunt, we had primarily discussed hunting elephant. That was frightening enough, but now we were actually 'thumbing our noses' at fate by spending the night suspended from a lashed tree house, intentionally, luring *simbas* to us. Denny and Edmond had come face to face with lions so aggressive that they did not hesitate to come into camp where numerous humans resided. I wondered about our sanity and what new lion 'tails' tomorrow would bring?

Stalking Elephant

Will expressed his growing concern to Francois. "Time is running out and I simply couldn't face the folks back home without taking an elephant." Consequently, the men determined to concentrate even harder on that task. The day was still young when we loaded up and headed out to find ourselves a big *tembo*. Soon afterwards, a large solitary bull with beautiful well-shaped ivory was spotted.

Edmond remarked to me, "Hunting such a seasoned bull is always challenging. It is one thing to track down a herd, with its cows and calves operating in their communal protocol. It is quite another matter to tackle a lone bull unfettered with family responsibilities. He is free to do his own thing, at his own whim and pleasure. Bulls only join the herd when the cows are in season. Once he has mated, he pushes off once more into his life of solitude."

Invigorated by this magnificent specimen, we excitedly piled out of our jeeps and followed the mammoth creature as he methodically foraged for food. I noticed him stripping the bark off trees and wondered why he would do such a thing. Edmond educated me on this practice. "This is not an uncommon practice in the dry season because the bark contains much needed moisture."

The stalk went well. After an hour or so, Will put an arrow into him but missed his mark by a mile. It turned out to be nothing more than a flesh wound with yellow feathers attached. As expected, the treasure-ladened bull took off at a fast clip. We had no choice but to follow suit, or risk losing him. We traveled for miles through the bush in a hurried rush that persisted beyond reason. A chase that ignored our need for rest and nourishment, for the more pressing need to keep up with the ever-moving giant. I struggled to keep up with the longer-legged men. When I could run no farther, I walked as fast as possible so as not to be left behind. Our safari leader's salient comments concerning chasing elephants came to mind. "Man must take several steps for each elephant's stride and, furthermore, we're more vulnerable to thicket, thorn, and temperature. And if white, we are susceptible as newborn babes to creatures that bite: mosquitoes, ants, tsetse flies."

I reflected on how I had progressed since my first long stalk. At first, I would fall, 'biting the dust' at least once a day. During the treks, Manyimancu was usually right behind me. Whenever I fell, he would politely offer me his hand, give me one of those I know you need help smiles, lift me up, and dust me off. By this point in the hunt, I was able to stay upright most of the time.

We trudged for miles through seven-foot-tall grasses, across rocky riverbeds, and into charred burned-out areas. We also traversed soil with numerous large holes made by heavy animals, dodged the thorn armed vegetation, and tramped through muddy *mkondos*. The exertion and heat sapped my energy reserves, my head ached, and my legs felt heavy and hard to lift.

The seasoned trackers had no problem following the animal. Most of the blood stains that they pointed out to me were about head height on trees and tall grasses. We found where the bull had stopped at a watering hole to smear mud on his side to seal off the surface wound. The bleeding lessened and tracking became more difficult which slowed our pace considerably. These were much welcomed breaks for my tired, over-taxed body. This grueling ordeal will be forever indelibly imprinted on my mind. I will never forget the hours spent chasing that bull elephant at 'full steam,' in 90-degree heat, over rough terrain.

Francois finally stopped the maddening push so we could replenish our empty water canteens. We threw off our backpacks and rushed over to a few small pools of water still visible alongside the sandy riverbed. I cupped my hands and drank. Now, I was not picky about what the water looked like or what was in it-just thirsty! I observed and felt a tiny bit comforted by the fact that the water holes had not adversely affected the tiny tadpoles swimming around in some of them. We doused our heads with the liquid. It was interesting to watch as the water trickled down my body making interesting patterns in my dirty clothing.

Japhet would surely earn his pay tomorrow trying to get our filthy clothing clean.

Francois removed his cloth hat, scooped up a hat full, then quickly plopped it back on his head. The liquid that did not run down his head and body comically squirted North, South, East and West out of his hat's four air vents. It looked like a cheap watered-down version of Rome's Trevi Fountain. Although I was half-dead from exhaustion, the comical sight made me laugh. Our Frenchman, who was never lacking in *savoir faire*, remained debonair even in these remote circumstances. In lieu of his usual large picnic cloth, he spread out a small *serviette,* napkin on the sand, for our tablecloth. I kidded, "Your safari operation never lacks class, no matter how small." We gobbled up every bit of my emergency rations. Each of us got a couple of bites of the sardines. Because we were starving, we savored every tiny morsel.

The natives used their hands to dig water holes in the sand to provide us with the H2O needed to refill our empty containers. Will assured me, "The sand acts as a natural filter so don't worry, the water is okay to drink." At this point, I was so desperately thirsty that he could have convinced me that the Brooklyn Bridge was a good buy. I took a long look at a cup full of the replacement water, which was the color of a strong cup of milk laden tea. As I hungrily gulped down a big mouthful, I hoped he was right. In retrospect, it is rare to find a place left in Africa where one can drink the water without getting bilharziasis, which is a disabling tropical disease caused by flatworms. Fortunately, in the Selous, one could drink with impunity from the sand filtered pools.

While resting I mentioned that I was intrigued by an elephant's trunk. Francois explained, "Their trunk is a prolongation of its upper lip and nose together. At the end of this enormous projection are two sensitive and flexible fingers. Trunks perform all the functions of a human's hand such as feeding, drinking, dusting, and fondling their loved ones. The average trunk measures about six feet long and tips the scale at 300 pounds." Edmond added, "Their elongated nose contains a boneless mass filled with 40,000 muscles and tendons. The trunk is not only strong and flexible, but also allows for control with great skill. This dexterity accounts for the fact that an elephant can pick up a single blade of grass as easily as a 600-pound log. These trunks are also used to magnify noise, and they scream, trumpet, grunt, rumble, and unbelievably, purr to express their emotions."

After an all too brief rest stop, we managed to get our beleaguered bodies back on our feet. It was hard to keep our spirits up as we searched for our bull. Due to tracking difficulties, many times the trackers temporarily lost sight of clues as to which way the elephant had gone. Eventually one of them would pick up a small shred of evidence and motion us onward. Tho delays in tracking were as welcomed by me as salvation is to sinners. I rested on the ground whenever possible, not caring what was beneath me. I knew full well by studious observation that every square inch of African soil is crawling with one thing or another. Having already garnered countless bites, I figured a few more would not make any difference.

On today's stalk I learned a valuable lesson the hard way. No matter how hot the weather is, it is insane to wear Bermuda shorts in the bush and had the scratches regarding my hypothesis to prove it.

I consoled myself with this thought; hunters are forged out of trails filled with trials. The title of hunter is not earned by simply turning over on ones cozy cot and realizing that the animal you are after, is so contemptuous of your prowess, as to stand in front of you and say, "Here I am…I'm all yours."

Toward late afternoon our search for the largest of all land animals lead us into a tsetse fly infested area. Brian was the only one wearing the proper apparel made of tightly woven mesh. The bites were painful, so I quickly took the insect repellant from my backpack and doused it liberally on Black and white. However, this expensive, highly touted deterrent did not phase our tormentors one iota. Every bite from the fiendish flying pests felt as if they were drilling for blood. In order to get some relief, Kisenga showed us his tried-and-true no cost remedy. He broke off and handed us several leafy tree branches to swat the pests away which proved remarkably effective.

Will told me later that he had taken one of those pesky flies, mashed it between his fingers and its wings remained intact. He marveled that it seemed indestructible and said, "Believe it or not, it flew away unscathed." Edmond smiled and said, "I'm not sure why we're so lucky, but the Selous has 20 different species of tsetse fly."

I thought that is one statistic I would not want others to know about.

Our somber safari guide then gave us some unwelcome news. "We've been on the elephant's trail way too long. We're miles from the vehicles, so we'll have to really hustle to get back to them before dark sets in." The thought of yet another lengthy, fast-paced walk was not what our exhausted group wanted to do hear much less do. After his unpopular pronouncement, Francois turned and began walking at such a brisk pace that the rest of us, who were near collapsing, could scarcely believe. Since our welfare was at stake, he knew what needed to be done to get his tired troopers back home safely. Just the thought of being in the dark amongst wild animals scared me sufficiently so that I found energy, in my 'reserve tank,' that I did not know existed.

I determined right then and there that before I left the Selous, my personal quest was to keep pace with that cocky Parisian.

As the setting sun sank lower on the horizon, it left ever lengthening shadows across our homeward path, much like hurdles at a track meet. Right at dusk, we crested a hill, and lo and behold, a familiar sight loomed below us in the distance. It was the banks of the Njenji! Francois compassionately allowed us to sit and rest once we reached the river's edge. Several of his men stumbled off into the blackness to collect our transportation.

I was curious as to how many miles we had walked. Francois answered, "*Mama,* in the bush, we measure in hours, not miles." After a long while, we saw the welcome lights of the jeeps moving steadily toward us. I will be eternally grateful for those benevolent men.

As we motored along, in the dark, the red hue of a fire off in the distance caught my attention. I asked Francois if he knew the cause of the fire. "I assume it was done by game personnel. This is the time of year when it's customary to burn."

The cooks had prepared a delicious antelope steak dinner for us with all the trimmings. Food had never tasted so good, but I was so tired it was an effort to chew, much less swallow. We were all near the zombie state. As soon as my head hit the pillow, I was fast asleep. I never raised it again until morning lit up the eastern horizon.

Francois' plan of attack for the new day, was to comb the area with every available man, leaving behind a skeletal staff in camp. We now referred to the bull we were seeking as 'Ol' Yeller' because of the yellow feathers that dangled from its side. This nickname came from a classic Walt Disney movie made in 1957, about a boy and his love for his dog, named Ol' Yeller.

After yesterday's long hard push, my legs felt as if they had turned into jelly. I decided to sit this one out. I stayed behind in camp to write and recuperate. I was like one of Brian's camera batteries that had run out of juice. Before the hunting party left Will promised me, "If we locate my 'feathered friend,' I'll send for you." I told him, "That's really sweet, but a crazy thing to do." Francois chimed in with "Yes, but we'll come after you anyway," then added with tongue in cheek, "unless he's gone as far as Dar-es-Salaam."

I had become an avid convert to living in a world without walls and was not at all reticent to stay behind in camp. This allowed me a rare opportunity to learn what things were like in camp during daylight hours, when we were traipsing around in the reserve. When I first arrived, I viewed the large number of workers as unnecessary. More American efficiency is what they need. But now, I had become more realistic about their need since primitive conditions made chores more time consuming.

The camp was a veritable beehive of activity. Kindling was gathered to keep a constant fire burning, and water had to be drawn and carried up from three large pools that had been dug in the river bottom behind our campsite. The water holes continuously filled with pure filtered water, which slowly seeped up through the layers of sand. Laundry was collected, hand washed, hung up to dry, then pressed with a heavy metal iron filled with hot coals. Japhet, used a small stiff brush to sweep out the floor of our sleeping quarters. He also made the beds and tidied them up. The cooks busied themselves with making bread, tenderizing the game meat, and preparing meals. The mechanics constantly tinkered with the jeeps making sure they were gassed up and in good working order.

During the day, whenever the camp personnel had a spare moment, they played soccer down on the dry riverbed behind camp. I was amazed at the dexterity these energetic amateur ball handlers exhibited.

The workers tents were pitched, underneath a clump of trees, a short distance from our campsite. I could hear a portable radio coming from their quarters as I worked on my journal. It was interesting to hear American Rock 'n Roll intermingled with their 'Jungle Top 40' tunes.

Rama, the cook, mentioned "Our camp supplies are almost gone, but if you'd like the cooks can prepare some spaghetti for your lunch." I agreed, envisioning a plate piled high with pasta drenched in a savory meat sauce. When my food arrived, my expectations burst like a bubble. A plate full of plain spaghetti noodles, and nothing more, brought me back to the reality of our empty cupboard.

During the afternoon, I caught sight of a group of cow elephants; the uncomely, but intrepid defenders of the family, with their young. As they started inching closer to camp, I remembered that all the men with rifles were out searching for Ol' Yeller. Fortunately, the potential threat never materialized because the camp workers bare-handedly ran after the elephants and 'shooed' them away. When they returned from chasing the large ladies away from our campsite, I asked, "What was the noise I heard when the elephants were close by?" Rama explained, "Madam, the sound is from the elephant's belly." I told him, "The rumbling noise reminded me of thunder before a rainstorm, except this noise was almost continuous." Some experts feel those sounds are a low growl of apprehension or a warning sound.

Mane Attraction

It was late afternoon when the jeeps rolled in behind the camp and Will yelled up at me, "Grab your gear, Jeannie. We're heading for the blind." Although they did not say so, I surmised that their search for Ol' Yeller had been fruitless. While heading for our destination, Will praised the trackers for their phenomenal ability to distinguish and track an elephant by its unique set of footprints. Francois added, "The pattern of creases in the joint above their foot also helps experts differentiate one elephant from another." Will said, "The trackers successfully tracked Ol' Yeller until he followed a well-worn game path down to the river's edge. The bank was damp with a myriad of animal footprints. This stymied the trackers, so we reluctantly gave up and came to get you."

Each turn of the jeep's wheels toward the blind, brought us ever closer to our expectations that Will's big lion would prove more cooperative tonight, than the elephant had been all day. Off in the distance we heard the riveting roar of a lion. Edmond whispered to me, "Believe it or not, you can hear a lion's roar within a 12-mile radius. It is their way of letting you feel their presence. Once you hear a commanding sound like that, it causes fear to vibrate throughout every nerve in your being." I wholeheartedly agreed that the lion had succeeded in getting my undivided attention.

We arrived at the blind just before dark. Francois advised us to be quiet. "A lion's night vision is equal to, or better than, its ample ability to see during the daylight." Soon after we got settled in the blind our diners came to check on their dinner reservations. The maître de found them their favorite spot in the dining room. Once informed that their nightly special was 'hoisted hindquarter' the ravenous diners roared their approval.

Tonight's episodes would prove to be the most 'hair raising' experiences thus far. Throughout the night, we heard frightening, unnerving noises beneath us, not unlike those emanating from a house of horrors on Halloween. It began with the rustling noise of leaves, followed by the sharp claws of ferocious feline's stripping meat off the bait. Next their muscular jaws began munching and crunching through flesh and bones. Occasionally, a skirmish broke out when some 'greedy gut' tried to take more than their 'lion's share' of the booty. Listening to all those nerve-racking sounds was like being wide awake during one's worst nightmare. Their frightful shenanigans sent shivers up and down my 'city slicker' spine.

Words uttered days earlier by our safari leader kept running through my frenzied mind. "A lion will fight for what he has, as well as, for what he needs; he is contemptuous of cowards and wary of his equals. But, make no mistake about it, he is not afraid. You can always trust a lion to be exactly what he is-an efficient killing machine. Over a distance of a few yards no animal, however fast, has greater speed than a charging lion. Their speed is faster than thought. Always faster than escape!"

I tried hard not to think of the list of 'what-ifs' this or that happened. Things like what if the lashing broke, or what if one of us rolled off the mattress and fell out of the tree. What if Will missed his mark and the lions turned on us. Just the thought of these possibilities was enough to send me to an early grave. The furious sounds, emanating from the voracious lions still ring in my ears, making it a night l shall NEVER forget!

At first light, Francois gestured for me to inch upward and watch a lioness taking her turn on the meat. Our overhead vantage point provided us a unique 'sneak peek' at this impressive creature. This rare close-up view made all the bugs, lumps in the mattress, and loss of sleep worth the effort. Francois nudged my arm, indicating he had something else to show me. My head swung to my far left. I could not believe what was slowly approaching. We breathlessly watched as her 500-pound companion cautiously strolled into view.

He sniffed the air flaunting his magnificent mane. His frightful jowls exposed teeth white as sun-cured bone. The momentum of his tail increased. His regal swagger left no doubt in anyone's mind that this majestic animal was undoubtedly the King of Beasts!

Will's slender body stood erect, bow in hand, breathily watching his lion approach the blind in the light of day. His bare-chested body tingled in excited anticipation. Unfortunately, the tree branches had only been cleared on the side facing the bait. His prize animal was approaching from another direction making a shot impossible. In silent frustration, he watched as the majestic specimen came within bow range.

Brian was capturing every exciting moment, but when his camera started and stopped it made a sound, which made me extremely nervous. I did not want the lion's attention diverted to a treetop kill. I knew we were tempting fate, but at the same time, thrilled to view the awesome couple at close range, without them being aware of it. After finishing her breakfast, the sire and his 'madam' sauntered out to bask in the sun on the riverbank. The fact that they had only ventured a short distance indicated that they were staking their claim on the meat and planned to return. But to Will's utter dismay, the pair were resting out of his bow range.

Through my field glasses, I watched the imposing couple sprawled out on the sand, enjoying their morning repose. Since the male was the biggest of Africa's carnivores, he was surely weary of patrolling and keeping tabs on the happenings in his kingdom; not unlike an emperor strolling through the halls of his palace. His long tail, with a distinctive black tuft at the tip, was stroking the grains of sand near where he lay. His massive mane varied in color from tawny to black. His huge frame was making an imprint in the sand, which would remain there once he left. The pair were not asleep, only idly resting.

At this exact moment, our dutiful camp staff were on their way to pick us up, but when they turned the bend in the river and spotted the lions they hurriedly retreated. After about an hour, the male lion slowly, but purposefully, raised himself while omitting a slight sound-a sigh. He turned in our direction contemplating the meat in a quiet premeditation. The furry lioness, aroused by her mate, stood, and shook the sand from herself, and lazily yawned. She began following her partner who was heading back to the tantalizing meat supply. Our hopes soared! Would Will get another chance at him? Suddenly our attention was diverted from the lions to the sound of a jeep.

Our minds silently screamed NO, NOT NOW-GO AWAY!

But the noise only grew louder. From his vantage point, the driver was unable to see the lions and supposed that they were gone. The closer the jeeps came; the redder Francois' face became. As the vehicles came into view, our flustered safari guide frantically tried waving them off, but it was everlastingly too late. If looks could kill, the driver would not be amongst the living.

To say the least, this was a heart-sinking experience, because when the lions heard the jeep they quickly disappeared. Fit to be tied over his staff's blunder, Francois was upset, because his personnel had disobeyed orders. Before coming close to the blind, they were supposed to stop at a designated place and wait for a 'go ahead' signal from their boss.

The remainder of the morning was spent relaxing in camp. About noon, I noticed the workers in the kitchen hunkered around a large pan, eating something, with their fingers. It resembled a firm mush made with white cornmeal. I mentioned that I would like to sample some of their traditional food. Francois encouraged me, "Go have a taste. It's good." I knelt in the circle beside my Black friends, flashed a big smile, before pulling off a small moist hunk. They watched to see my reaction. I enjoyed my taste of *'ugali,'* a maize flour and water dish that thickens into a stiff porridge. However, I found the African staple food rather bland. When I pinched off a second piece, they had me dip it into a delicious sauce. It was apparent that my willingness to try their food pleased them.

According to our French authority on Africa, "The Wandarobo trackers are part of the Maasai, a tribe which raises livestock for their livelihood. They live in a territory that overlaps the boundary between Kenya and Tanzania. The Maasai live alongside wild animals but have an aversion to eating game and bird. They prefer to drink a concoction of milk and blood. The blood is extracted by puncturing a cow's jugular vein with a sharp pointed object. After the bloodletting, the wound is closed off with a bit of mud."

"Surely," I protested "they eat the meat of their cattle." Francois adamantly insisted, "They do not eat the meat, only its milk and blood, but they do supplement their diet with fruits and grains." He felt this unusual diet is the secret behind their strength and endurance. "These tribesmen are dependent on their cattle, hence the greeting they give to their friends when they meet in the savannah is, "I hope your cows are well."

"Their beliefs indicate that when sky and land were separated, *Ngai*, their God, sent them cattle. The Maasai conclude that since the cow is linked to the land, both are sacred. They will not betray God's gift to them by slaughtering cattle or piercing the ground to cultivate it. They do not go against this tradition. Not even to bury their dead, but instead leave them for the wild animals."

I queried, "Do they dig water wells?" Francois insisted, "No, but the government has provided them with wells, but the majority of the Maasai prefer to use the streams and natural water sources." From time to time, I would look at our trackers and envision them clasping a gourd of blood and milk, looking heavenward, and chanting in low voices as they give thanks to God.

One of the drivers who arrived from the main camp told Francois that the black leopard had finished off its bait. This meant that fresh meat was urgently needed to keep its interest piqued. I assumed that black leopards were commonplace, but Edmond said, "*Mama,* only one out of every 600 leopards are black."

We hopped into the jeeps and headed toward the watering hole of some hippopotamuses who lived nearby. Their large bodies would provide us an ample meat supply for both sites. Sure enough, the big water hole was monopolized by a pod of stout barrel-shaped hippos. Will stood primed and ready to get a shot. The men did everything but stand on their heads, including throwing rocks and sticks into the water, attempting to separate one from the pod. But they kept their wits about them and stayed put in their watery fortress.

During these futile attempts Francois pointed out, "The Selous has one of the world's largest known populations of hippopotamuses. They are not light eaters. These big guys require about 130 pounds of vegetable matter each day to maintain their 'figures'. After gorging themselves, they sleep 16 hours a day." I asked, "How much do they weigh?" The answer was they average from 2,500 to 3,000 pounds.

I found the water lovers fascinating and humorous to watch. After staying submerged for 5 minutes, they surfaced for air and made a blowing noise while simultaneously twitching their ears around. Edmond explained, "Don't be fooled by how harmless they look in the water. They are the third largest land animal. Although these river pigs can weigh as much as 5,800 pounds, they can run as fast as a human being." Francois astounded us by saying, "Yes, and in addition to their unbelievable speed, they also have immense jaws full of long shearing ivory teeth. They kill more people in Africa than any other land animal. They are the most ferocious when cut off from their water sanctuaries. No animal dares to attack an adult hippo, however, crocs, hyenas, and lions sometimes kill their young."

As one of the larger hippos popped up for air, Denny turned to Brian and sarcastically stated, "That big guy over there reminds me a little of you. What do you think?" Brian pretending to be offended, offered this snide comment. "Hey turkey, be careful. Us big guys love snacking on skinny little wise guys." After a good laugh, we left the seemingly unperturbed hippos ducking in and out of the water.

When we arrived back in camp, Francois got an emergency message from main camp on the two-way radio. I prayed that it was not concerning our family. To relieve our concerns, Francois indicated he had just received word that our driver is to take a jeep and return immediately to main camp. His young son has just died."

On safari, we were constantly dealing with killing and death, but this tragedy hit us all hard. A sense of melancholy permeated the camp. We felt empathy for his terrible loss because all of us were parents, and our friend had just lost his precious child. In a tender moment, Francois sympathized with his driver, gave him some money, and sent him home to be with his family. "The mortality rate of African children," our white hunter explained, "is extremely high and is particularly so during the rainy season, when diseases are even more prevalent."

Unexpected Reunion

The adage, time flies when you're having fun, truly applied to this three-week endeavor. With only seven days left to hunt, Will's desire to get his elephant grew stronger by the day.

Before sunset, we stopped by our tree blind to make some much needed 'home improvements.' Francois and Kisenga scurried up into the blind and threw out the dead foliage which had served as camouflage. Now it was nothing more than a noisy nuisance. At my suggestion, the workers placed the old dry branches in and around the bait. Hopefully, the crackle of the dry leaves would act as an alarm system to let us know when the lions were nearby. They also added fresh foliage and pruned any tree branches that could possibly hinder Will's shooting possibilities. Kisenga then descended the tree and indicated that Francois was ready for us to come up and join him.

This was my third night in the blind, so I felt a bit more comfortable undertaking the tedious ascent. I sat down next to Francois, and while I untied my shoelaces he leaned my way and whispered, "The camp personnel think you're something special."

I asked, "Why?"

"Because they have never seen a woman in a lion blind, and for that matter neither have I."

So, the truth was out. I was the first woman to stay in a lion blind! I had mistakenly supposed that if physically able everyone did it.

Tonight was Will, Brian, and Francois' sixth night in the treehouse. The cook had sent along a rice mixture in a plastic container. We all agreed that a can of tuna would perk up the otherwise dull dish. I retrieved the tin from my backpack and carefully opened it. I needed to get rid of the excess oil before adding it to the rice. Francois pointed for me to pour the smelly liquid down the tree trunk. As I reluctantly did so, a statement he had made earlier flashed through my mind.

Lions are more intelligent than some men, and more courageous than most.

I fervently hoped these carnivores were not the inquisitive type who would investigate the source of the unusual odor oozing down our tree trunk. I did not want to attract their attention to some 'bigger fish' up in the tree.

This night's occurrences were about the same as the others, with the exception that we experienced some gentle gusts of wind. Whenever the breeze rustled the leaves, it allowed us to move around more freely without fear of being detected. The disadvantage was that it also brought the full fury of the stinking lure.

Suddenly the roar of a lion in the vicinity rolled against the stillness of the night. I listened in horrified anticipation. Shortly thereafter, several lions came calling. When nearing our tree, they obviously smelled the fishy odor and came to sniff out its source. My blood ran cold! Oh, how sorry I was that I had listened to Francois.

Were they on to us? I knew house cats loved fish, so perhaps these big cats would like a change of menu like "tuna a la tree."

Fortunately, numerous hyenas had gathered nearby. The frustrated group began whimpering loudly in hopes of getting a taste of the tempting meat. Their aggressive actions turned the lion's attention away from us and onto the bait. The lions fear of losing it, caused them to ravenously tear into and polish it off. The hungry hyenas were now out of luck because the lions literally 'licked the platter clean' before pushing off elsewhere.

The next day, my back was feeling the effects of spending three consecutive nights sleeping on flooring made of branches. If one were looking for comfortable accommodations in an insect-free establishment, I would not recommend the 'Selous Treetop Towers.'

An enterprising chiropractor could have made a fortune by setting up shop at the base of our tree.

Breakfast consisted of served eggs and toast with the inevitable sprinkling of sand. Afterwards Francois herded 12 of us into the jeeps, gave his husky *'twende'* command, and we embarked on another adventure. We never doubted for one minute that our Frenchman did not have everything under control. He had a knack for extracting the best efforts from all of us. To his clients, he gave his genius and his energy. He gave the workers his help and understanding. At appropriate times, he would converse and joke around with them in fluent Swahili. He had lived amongst the native culture long enough to understand their seemingly uncivilized ways, at least, by white man's standards. Francois' mind was uncluttered by the notion that the white man's civilization had nothing to learn from the Black man's way of life. He respected the spirit of their traditions, their physical stamina, and their uncanny tracking ability.

We drove right past our well-fed lions lounging along the riverbank observing our procession of jeeps rolling by. One lion swung its tail in high arcs as if to wave at us through the tall wispy grass. I jokingly postulated as to what our felines might be thinking.

Good luck hunting today. Get us something good to eat. We'll be over for dinner after dark.

A short while later, Will and his guide, made a stalk on a couple of wildebeest. This was a rare opportunity because usually Kisenga and the other trackers were with them. In the hunter's absence, Brian, Denny, and I got our only spare time together during daylight hours. We used it to make much-needed filler material for the forthcoming documentary. Brian had the trackers reenact some of the scenes from the hunt, so he could get close-ups of their expressions and movements. They cooperated beautifully considering we could only communicate via sign language. My job was to hold a large silver folding screen close to the tracker's faces. Brian explained, "A Black's face is difficult to photograph, and this screen helps reflect the maximum lighting for capturing their facial features."

Long before we had finished filming, our driver got a signal from the empty-handed hunters, who had decided it was pointless to waste more time on the easily spooked antelopes. As it turned out, it was a good thing they quit when they did, because not long afterwards a truly miraculous incident occurred.

Grey giants, who roam this fascinating land, were spotted up ahead. Initially, Francois paid little heed to them. When Will insisted that one of the elephants had nice, long tusks like Ol' Yeller's, the safari leader took a second look.

He gasped!

At about the same time, Will, who was busily glassing the tuskers, spotted the yellow fletching's of his arrow adorning the elephant's hide.

He joyfully proclaimed, "It's Ol' Yeller. This is my lucky day!" And thus, it was that our eyes were once again cheered by the sight of Ol' Yeller.

The hunters sprang into action. Will grabbed his bow that by now was as much a part of him as the sinews of his body. We followed Ol' Yeller's every move down a dung littered path made by him and the three hulks accompanying him. After several miles, the bulls stopped to do what all elephants do every chance they get-eat. We climbed up on top of a high bluff where we could easily keep an eye on him and his companions. Peering off the high escarpment at the elephants below, made them seem less than life size. It felt like what I was beholding was wonderful, but not real.

We decided to follow the elephant's lead and have some lunch. We had learned from experience that when an elephant is on the move, there is no time to piddle around picnicking.

After eating, Will went to practice his shooting. Brian and Denny took a siesta under a shady tree. Francois came over to where I was writing. "What are you thinking, *Mama?*" His question touched my heart because nobody had ever cared enough to ask about my inner thoughts and feelings. "Oh, I'm curious about what elephants do to amuse themselves when hunters aren't hot on their trail." Francois sat down next to me and quietly explained, "In places where they're liable to be disturbed, they stay hidden in the trees. During the night they venture out to feed in open spaces and thinly wooded areas. In this dry weather they visit the rivers every night. In cooler, cloudy seasons they drink less frequently. At dawn, they retire to the densest cover within reach, usually in the long-needled 'wait-a-bit' thorn thickets."

I asked him why there was a layer of something resembling mud covering the bark of the tree against which I was resting. Francois took great pleasure in explaining to this innocent neophyte, "The dirt-looking residue is left by termites." I gave him the response I am sure he was expecting, when I blurted out, "You mean I'm leaning up against a termite infested tree!" With a big grin on his face, he affirmed my suspicions. We joked that if I stayed there much longer, I might come away with a new backless design in safari attire. "In fact," I told him, "I've already had a run in with those little eating machines. The other day, I washed the mud off my leather shoes and left them to dry, turned upside down, on the wooden poles of my wash basin. When I retrieved them, two days later, I was shocked to find that the termites had greedily gnawed the insides out of both shoes. He seemed to enjoy my telling of the unfortunate run in with the tenacious terminates.

During our conversation, the lion blind was mentioned. Francois told me that he seriously was not aware of any woman who had slept in a blind above the lions. He confided in me saying, "Some men refuse to stay up in the tree stand because, they claim they can't stomach the wretched smell of rotting meat." I assured him that it was not my favorite aroma either. "To get my mind off the smell, I focus my attention on something more pleasant like the world's biggest and best heavenly light show."

I got a chance to ask him if most women participate in the hunt to the extent I had done. He emphatically retorted with a resounding, "Definitely not! Many clients simply do not have the physical stamina to track an animal as you have done. Furthermore, none of the gun hunters, and most certainly, none of their spouses have made the number of lengthy stalks that you have done almost daily. Bow hunters must stalk and get in close for a shot, whereas gun hunters can drop an animal from a long way off, using the high-powered scopes on their rifles." With a tone of disgust in his voice, I was flabbergasted to learn that some hunters even lack the guts to leave the safety of their jeep.

We could have talked for hours, but our conversation abruptly ended when the ever-observant Kisenga came running towards us. He pointed to Ol' Yeller and his cohorts, who were high tailing it over to the opposite bank, with their fan-like ears flapping as fast as their feet could carry them. This unforeseen turn of events had to be dealt with quickly in order to catch the tuskers. In a split second, our circumstances changed from serenity to bedlam. Luckily, Will had just returned from his practice session.

Francois darted over to the edge of the high bluff looking for a suitable exit. After locating one he and Will plunged over the hill. Our adventurers left with such gusto, as to lead me to believe that they would greet doomsday with nothing but a blink. Kisenga frantically motioned for me to follow him over the side, so I grabbed my backpack and slid down the 50-foot ravine without regard for life or limb. I mis-timed my descent and almost landed right on top of his head. When the dust settled from the avalanche of humanity traversing the hill, fortunately, we were all in one piece. I located my pack and my composure and began chasing the elephants. Will, Francois, and Kisenga were now sprinting in pursuit of the fleeing pachyderms. I did my best to keep up with the adrenalin charged males but running on this hot sandy surface was exhausting.

Halfway across the Njenji, I started running out of steam. I steadily dropped farther and farther behind but was still considerably ahead of the rest of the group.

Just as I reached the opposite bank, I heard a noise coming up from behind me, which scared me to death. I turned to see what it was. Thankfully, it was Brian. He was toting the heavy 50 1b. camera and all its attendant gear strapped to his sweat-soaked body. He ran past me without uttering a word, as if he were on assignment to film East Africa sliding into the Indian Ocean. I kept up with him until we got into the seven-foot-tall grasses, then I suddenly lost sight of him. The grasses had swallowed Brian whole like Jonah disappearing inside the belly of the large fish.

I was lost, all alone, and without my 'mama protector'!

A helpless unnerving feeling of pure unadulterated panic came over me! I stood frozen in fear hoping someone friendly would find me before some animal did. Under these tense circumstances, seconds seemed like hours. My prayers pleading for help were as fervent as any I had ever uttered before or since. Soon I heard movement in the weeds.

Was it friend or foe?

To my immense joy, it was Denny and five others. Once the men showed up, our game scout, Manyimancu, tried his best to pick up a clue as to which way the elephant and the hunters had gone. It became abundantly clear that we had lost them. Now I did not feel so bad about my unsuccessful attempts to follow them.

Some of the men climbed up in trees to try and locate them.

They saw nothing.

The natives tried signaling the other members of our party by making whistling noises.

No response.

Chapter 17

Denny and I were frustrated and wondered what was happening with the elephant and his pursuers as we waited by the jeeps with the others.

Perilous Pursuit

Africa is a continent of extremes that breeds animals tough enough to adapt to its demands on them, particularly the weather. Today, in our little corner of the world, the sky was devoid of clouds and the sun was beating down with a vengeance. So much so that, while resting under a clump of trees, Denny and I witnessed heat waves rising from the burning sand in the riverbed. On top of that, we were feeling a burning desire to get back in the action.

Denny told me, "The rainy season here occurs between December and April. Throughout December, storms become more frequent. The game begins moving away from the rivers, leaving the crocs and hippos behind in peaceful isolation. Mercifully, each year the rivers overflow and revive the scorched earth. During the seasonal flooding of the Rufiji River, the place where we are sitting will easily be under six feet of water. The soils are subject to erosion during the heavy rains. We see evidence of that in the steep banks of the *mkondos*." The flooding seemed inconceivable as hot and dry as it is now.

It was a mystery to me why the heavy elephants did not get bogged down in the sand and mud. Denny educated me on the subject. "They can walk on their toes! Part of each foot contains a tough spongy material which acts as a cushion. These unique pads help support their weight. Their big feet have the remarkable ability to shrink. If their feet sink into the terrain, they can easily pull it out because their feet become smaller as they lift them."

"Wow, that's truly astounding!"

As we swallowed the last drops of our drink, low and behold, what came into sight turned our disappointment into delight. Some 400 yards upstream, we saw several *'tembo'* crossing the river led by none other than-Ol' Yeller! Next came Will and his 'shadows.' As always, I was relieved to see that the men were still alive.

Denny was overjoyed at our unexpected chance to rejoin the hunt. He jumped up, wiped the sweat off his forehead, then threw on his hat. He enthusiastically announced, "By golly, this time they're not going to lose me." He and I raced to catch up with them. My strides were no match for Denny's long, lanky legs. He soon disappeared up the bank and into the brush in a rush of excitement seldom seen in a man his age. In my effort to keep up, I felt like Alice in Wonderland following the fast-moving White Rabbit. I was all alone with no tracking ability, no compass, and no weapon. Stymied, I was forced to wait until the rest of our party caught up with me. This time Manyimancu was able to ferret out which way they had gone. Soon our entire group was reunited.

But not for long.

We ran, in single file, through the rough grasses. The big bull, and his three traveling companions knew they were being chased by some very persistent pursuers. They would occasionally stop and glance over their shoulders, then scurry off once again.

It was then that a very unfortunate incident occurred.

While breathlessly running, I noticed something moving under a tree up ahead. I took a second look. It moved again and this time it took shape. It was a mother protecting her young offspring. Her ears twitched nervously. Francois could see that our situation was '*hatari sana,*' extremely dangerous, because cows with their young are always on the defense. For safety sake, everyone except Will and the trackers were sent back to the jeeps. While retreating, I looked to my right and froze in my tracks. One of the older 'nannies' had us on her radar and there was fire in her eyes. We would be no match for this 12,000-pounds of womanhood with an intense mothering instinct. Her ears were flaring, indicating she was mad as a hornet.

An unpleasant hush fell over the bush. I did not have to be told that our situation was as serious as it gets.

On a hand signal from Manyimancu, we began stepping slowly backwards as quietly and motionlessly as humanly possible. We were careful not to run or take our eyes off the fuming female because the slightest thing would trigger an unwelcome reaction. Cremation would be superfluous if they decided to charge!

Following our withdrawal maneuvers, Manyimancu quickly started a fire to place a safety-barrier between us and the 'womenfolk.' The flames devoured the dry brittle grass with an insatiable hunger. Now, protected by the smoke screen and the sounds of the crackling fire, we did some fast footwork to get away from the fire and the disgruntled ladies. Fortunately, we all came away unscathed, but we were acutely aware that this harrowing experience had been our closest call thus far. Once again, we had cheated death!

When Brian and Denny got back to the jeeps, they cooled their weary, sweat-soaked bodies by downing numerous soft drinks. Denny unstrapped the sound equipment and began digging a deep hole in the sand. Next, he rolled up his pants, exposing two lily-white legs, then removed his shoes and socks. Once the hole filled with water, he plopped his tired feet into his makeshift foot bath.

Brian stretched out on the sand and used a heap of Denny's sand diggings for a pillow. Our camera buff turned to me and commented, "Jean, up until now I've enjoyed this safari, but today I could sense the danger and tension emanating from Francois and his trackers." Then he quickly added, "Quite honestly, I've had enough! Today, it's become crystal clear that killing an elephant has become more important than sanity."

I knew he was probably right. I tried calming him by saying how determined hunters that have not reached their goal get desperate and take unwise risks. The reclining giant raised himself up on his elbow and said emphatically, "What they're doing has surpassed determination. In my opinion it borders on lunacy!"

One would be hard pressed to classify Brian as a sissy. He was an ex-college football star who had a full ride academic scholarship for the University of the Pacific. Shaking his head in disbelief at the hunters' stamina, he openly admitted, "I may be younger, but those two guys have put me 'in the shade' on this safari."

I had the distinct feeling that if Brian could have found a way home, he would be long gone.

After a well-deserved recuperation period, we caught sight of our men up ahead motioning to us for a ride. As we drew closer, our hitchhikers were acting unusually mischievous, not unlike young boys who had just skipped school.

What had happened to make them act this way?

Their jovial jesters interspersed with loud laughter led us to surmise that they had gotten Ol' Yeller. The tale the elephant enthusiasts unfolded, made Brian's comment concerning their 'devil-may-care' attitude seem clairvoyant.

Tusker's Revenge

After Francois had sent us back to the jeeps for safety sake, Ol' Yeller separated himself from his companions. He had apparently decided it was time to put an end to this game of hide and seek. The fed-up tusker suddenly spun around leaving only 80-yards between him and his pursuers. He defiantly stood his ground in a battle of 'wills.'

Quickly turning to his African expert, Will frantically inquired, "What now?" Francois' answer was downright shocking. "We're going to keep the pressure on him by moving up to within 30-yards so you can get a good shot."

Will, looking for a way out of this perilous predicament, said "This bull is obviously fed up and ready to fight. What will he do when we keep pressing him?"

Francois matter-of-factly stated, "Charge, of course!"

Will was not overjoyed at what he heard. He later admitted that at this point, he'd had his bellyful of elephants.

In a cavalier manner, the safari leader whispered, "Come on," to his hesitant client who had not moved an inch. Francois then took about 10 steps toward Ol' Yeller who was intently observing their every move.

Will said he was so scared that his feet felt like lead anchors which refused to budge. When Francois noticed that Will had not made any forward progress, he turned and flashed him a nasty, humiliating look. From then on, for every three or four strides Francois took, the reluctant archer followed with one or two baby steps and continued lagging behind. After several more scowls, Will finally closed the gap to save face, rather than from a desire to tackle the big bull. The bowman's enthusiasm for tackling elephants had dried up.

With each step, Will said to himself, "I'll inch a bit closer and see just how crazy this fearless Frenchman really is."

He pussyfooted toward Ol' Yeller for his moment of truth. The trackers later told us that the belligerent bull who was holding his ground would gather grass with his trunk as if eating. Actually, he never put anything into his mouth, but instead just tossed it over his shoulder while keeping his eyes on the advancing interlopers.

Francois stopped about 45 yards from the bull whose size resembled a huge cement mixer. He quietly instructed Will, "Crawl to within 30-yards and take your shoot." Will was dumbfounded at his seemingly incongruous instructions. "Francois, you know even Superman can't pull this 90-pound bow in the kneeling position. Besides that, after my shot, I can't run on my knees." This evoked a faint smile from his buddy who acquiesced and said, "Well, then do what you want."

Will told Francois, "See those saplings about 5 yards away? I'll draw my bow from behind them. They'll give me some cover." Before he left Francois' side, he enquired almost childishly, "What should I do once I've completed my shot?" His teacher turned toward his anxious pupil, and possibly soon to be demised archer, and answered, "Look my way and I'll give you further instructions."

Will, intent on proving his metal, worked himself into position behind the small trees. Using them for cover, he pulled back the heavy bow and with all the energy his adrenalin-filled body could muster, stepped out, and let his arrow fly.

He never even stopped to see if he hit his target. He whirled around in time to see all the trackers 'tearing up the turf,' scampering up the hill behind him. Will sensed, and rightfully so, that there was no need to wait for Francois' coaching tips. He instinctively started running for dear life. Sure enough, after he had taken two or three steps, the body of the enraged bull began swaying. With outspread ears, his trunk held high, he let out a scream.

A shill, cold as winter's wind, type of scream. Terrifying enough to hold you where you stood. Like deadly fingers clutching your throat.

This was unlike the daily doses of danger we had experienced thus far. NO, this signaled an eminent deadly charge that meant BIG trouble for all in sight! Ol' Yeller was gathering momentum to mow down his assailants. In a surging flow of mounting fury, Ol' Yeller was off in a typhoon of crumpled vegetation.

Trees fell to the ground like toothpicks!

Terra firma shook!

The tables were now turned as the enraged bull was HOT on their trail! While running his fastest, He felt sure that at any moment, he would be snatched up in Yeller's trunk or speared like a party hors d'oeuvre by his deadly ivory.

Will ran about 50 yards before Francois caught up with him, moving as fast as his shorter but younger legs could carry him. After running about 80 yards, Francois knew he could not keep up this pace. While still on a dead run, the white hunter did something completely unexpected. He reached up, grabbed the cloth hat off his head, and defiantly threw it down on the ground, as if it were a gauntlet.

Lo and behold, 'the hat challenge' got Ol' Yeller's attention. The bruiser stopped his charge and started taking out his pent-up anger by stomping on the hat. This diversion gave Francois enough time to run an additional 10 yards and jump behind a tree. He cocked his gun and was ready to blast away if necessary. Thankfully Ol' Yeller stormed off through the trees, convinced he had again outsmarted his irksome enemies.

When Ol 'Yeller began his charge, Kisenga with his years of experience, knew that he needed to immediately seek cover or be mowed down by the big grey widow maker. He ran halfway up the hill but began running out of steam, so he curled up in a hole for protection. The younger trackers cleared the top of the hill. When everyone saw that the 'coast was clear,' they rejoined the hunters.

Francois decided it was safe to return to the scene of the skirmish, retrieve his freshly flattened chapeau, and survey the damage. The landscape looked like an army tank had driven down through the bush. He had flattened everything in his path. Unfortunately, Brian had not been along to record this thrilling incident as he too had been sent back to safety with the rest of us.

The adventuresome men had seen enough excitement for one day, so they whistled, and we drove down to pick them up.

Henceforth, I teasingly referred to Francois as the 'Mad Hatter.'

Evasion Game

The next morning, Denny was sent to the main camp to find out why we were two days overdue getting our desperately needed supplies --food and Brian's camera batteries. Our camera expert was feeling anxious because he was using his last battery, which could go dead at any time. While at Kibaoni, Denny was to schedule a charter flight to pick us up next Thursday afternoon.

I stayed in camp while the men went back to see if they could locate Ol' Yeller's whereabouts. In their absence, I chuckled to myself as I recalled what Will had said at the outset of our trip. "I sure hope you won't be too bored because of the long time we'll be away from civilization." It was true that this was a lengthy sojourn, but I had become so enamored with all that Africa had to offer that time was simply flying by. I was relishing the extraordinary opportunity to be amongst Earth's most unique wildlife.

As to our initial concerns about our white hunter and his operation, we could not have been more pleased. From Will's perspective, Francois was a hardworking, knowledgeable guide. I found him to be witty, an interesting conservationist, and considerate.

After lunch Langael startled me by unexpectedly coming up beside me at the table where I was working. His appearance was somewhat frightening because of his crossed eye and protruding front teeth. He had something in his hands that he wanted me to see. He placed before me two pieces of beautifully handcrafted jewelry. One was an adjustable elephant's tail bracelet. The other bracelet was made of a callous off of an elephant's foot. At first, I thought he was trying to sell me his wares, but in broken English he shyly said, "For you, *Mama Mshale*."

I was very touched by this native's kind generosity and humbled that the staff cared enough to make me these priceless treasures. I was also pleased concerning my acceptance by the men in our party. Throughout the hunt, Will kept telling me how glad he was that I had come along, especially right after I had just rubbed his aching shoulders. Denny mentioned several times, while on our long stalks, that I kept up remarkably well. Francois had commented that I was a very patient woman.

About 5 p.m., a jeep returned with Brian's freshly charged batteries and our much-needed food supplies. I was hoping for a change of menu and excited to see some new varieties of fresh produce. I felt I had eaten so many eggs that I was beginning to cackle. The rice, canned meats and fish, and boiled potatoes were also getting monotonous. From time to time, Denny and Brian commiserated about how much ice cream and chocolate chip cookies they would devour once they got home. I must admit, I would have 'killed' for some hot, crunchy popcorn.

A little later, Denny's jeep pulled up. Accompanying him was Carlo, the 17-year-old son of an Italian professional game guide. Carlo had followed in his father's footsteps and was now classified as a white hunter. He and his client had just completed their hunt in another hunting district. Being naturally curious about how our unorthodox hunt was progressing, the tall, slender youth came for a visit. He offered his assistance when he heard we were still 'elephantless.'

Francois and his discouraged group rolled in as the sun was setting, saying they had not seen 'hide nor hair' of Ol' Yeller. This grey ghost had simply vanished. He seemingly had the longevity of a cat with nine lives.

When Denny and Carlo arrived from the main camp, they shared a frightful encounter with a menacing snake. Their jeep had driven close to a black mamba, one of the deadliest snakes in Central Africa. Carlo said that this snake can raise itself up, 4 or 5 feet, like its hooded kinsman, the cobra. This snake can also move forward while in the upright position making it possible to strike humans in open safari vehicles.

"What do they look like?" I queried. Carlo fielded my question in broken English with his darling Italian accent. "They real long, 'bout 14-feet and real skinny. Looka like a whip. They slither quicka in da trees. On da ground they movea fast, 'bout 14 miles an hour. If you get bita, you be a goner less you getta injection."

Will asked Francois, "Do you have the snake serum and needles with you?"

"Yes, in my bag that I carry wherever I go, and there is also another one here in camp."

Will said, "You're pretty serious about these snakes." The bush veteran said in a serious tone, "One must be prepared. This is dangerous country."

Several times, during our treks, I had noticed holes in the ground and had asked the men what lived there. Now I could better relate to the venomous viper they had mentioned and hoped we would not pass another one of their dangerous dwellings.

The next day, Francois enlisted the help of his Italian counterpart. "We need some fresh lion bait, preferably hippo meat, because our supply is gone."

We left camp by 7 a.m. in search of something quite different than wild game. Much to my chagrin, our first stop was to check in and around the lion blind for, of all things, my wristwatch. Yes, I had been advised not to wear it on safari but knowing what time it was seemed infinitely more important than heeding Will's good advice. We visited other locations where we had previously stopped, but all efforts to locate my costly timepiece proved unsuccessful. I hoped I would not have to listen to a steady diet of 'I told you so's' the rest of my days over this foolish blunder.

We then pursued our least favorite pastime of driving along the riverbeds looking for Ol' Yeller. We noticed that the animals were not congregating down at the water's edge today. I wanted to know what happened to all the wildlife. Francois answered, "The reason the animals haven't come to drink at the river is twofold. One is due to cooler temperatures caused by overcast conditions somewhere in the area. The other reason is that rain has replenished some watering holes." We had purposely chosen to hunt the Selous during the dry season. As Will so aptly put it, "Having the game concentrated around water is the only chance I have of seeing game in this vast area."

Francois finally called a halt to our incessant searching for Ol' Yeller. He instructed the driver to turn around and we headed to a beautiful park-like setting for lunch. During the meal, Francois casually mentioned, that today, October 4, was the birthday of his patron saint, St. Francis of Assisi. "In two days, I will turn 38 years old".

I made a mental note that if possible, we would somehow celebrate his birthday.

I shall always cherish the spicy stories served up by our kingly, French adventurer in the shade of whatever tree did serve as his throne room. Today our storyteller talked about the yearly migration of the Nuba tribe in the Sudan. "When the tribesmen reach the Nile River, their wary animals balk at crossing." He turned the can opener a bit slower around the tuna tin as he said, "It's no wonder they're hesitant; it's teaming with huge, hungry crocodiles!" To help us mentally picture how massive the crocs were, our guide described them as being the length of our jeeps and as wide as the camp's dining table. His description of their situation gave us a healthy respect for the magnitude of the tribe's problem in crossing the wide waters of the Nile.

"Some of the valiant men must dive into the treacherous waters to coax their cattle into swimming across. While the men and animals are crossing, the tribe's women and children line the banks. They beat their drums and shout, attempting to divert the croc's attention away from their loved ones and livestock." While salting his boiled egg, Francois spoke with admiration about the native's bravery. "Every now and then, some of those courageous men and their livestock drop out of sight, as they are dragged underneath in the jaws of hungry crocodiles." I thought that would be so hard to watch and even harder to do.

After our rest and Will's practice shooting session, we continued searching Ol' Yeller's usual hangouts. To break the monotony, I asked Francois to tell me about his favorite tribe. He indicated, "I truly don't have a particular preference." I pointed to the Wandarobo trackers in the back of our rig and said, "your favorites are these 'Wandering Robos.' He liked my play on words, so from time to time, we had fun referring to his men in this manner.

The fun and games ended when an elephant was sited. Will was unimpressed with the size of its ivory and was not keen on tackling another 'tembo' so late in the day. He readily admitted, "I'm pretty worn out from hunting all day and staying in the lion blind most every night." His feelings concerning elephants had swung like a pendulum, from overconfidence on his first encounter with a bull, to being reluctant to tackle this one. He confided in Francois and me, 'I've never run across an animal I couldn't get the best of, one way or another."

Had 'Big Bwana' met his match?

Francois offered his client this kind observation. "Elephants aren't dumb. You can almost compare their intelligence to that of an average human. They're less agile and physically adaptable, having developed their bodies in one direction and their brains in another." He raised his sunglasses to look at us and winked while saying, "We humans, on the other hand, draw both the winning ticket and the matching stub."

Carlo and his driver then caught up to us with the good news that he had successfully secured the needed hippo meat and had strung its hindquarters up as bait. We had high hopes for the lion hunter since no self-respecting lion could pass up tonight's special– 'hunks of hippo.'

Chapter 21

The Mad Hatter's Celebration

During breakfast, Francois reported the unwelcomed news that only hyenas had visited the bait sight. "It's not good to have so many hyenas around the meat. They hunt in packs, and even a lion must beware of them, especially a lioness with young to protect."

"Oh, by the way Brian, a snake visited the blind last night over in the area where you usually sleep. He was there keeping your bed warm until you get back."

Brian scoffed, "That must have been a whopper of a snake to be able to keep my spot warm."

Francois seemed to delight in the fact that he had elicited such a funny retort out of the cameraman. It would be an understatement to say that I was glad I had not stayed in the blind that night. Admittedly, it would have been impossible for me to have kept calm, cool, and collected, much less quiet, amongst such dreadful company.

Today our safari leader headed the jeep convoy back to Ol' Yeller's stomping grounds. We drove for hours but did not have any luck locating our evasive elephant.

It is said that an elephant never forgets. Could it be that our elephant had forgotten where he was supposed to be?

Throughout the reserve, there were abundant indications of a large elephant population. It was especially true where we were camped. Evidenced in the bark being stripped from trees, in the smashed branches, and uprooted trees, not to mention huge piles of droppings dotting the landscape.

I asked, "What happens to the aged and diseased elephants?" This sparked a discussion about the controversial superstition concerning elephants disposing of their dead in secret burial grounds. Francois speculated, "In support of this unsubstantiated belief, is the fact that an elephant's body, unless trapped or shot in his tracks, has rarely been found." Edmond commented, "For years natives and white settlers alike have supported the legend, if in fact it is legend, that elephant carry their sick and wounded for miles if necessary, to get them out of harm's way."

Had Ol' Yeller been whisked off to some mysterious location?

While peeling his orange, Francois stretched himself out on the ground and brought up another intriguing subject. "According to Maasai traditions, single males in order to marry must first prove their manhood with a lion kill. Once a lion is spotted, the valiant warriors form a circle. Naturally, men with matrimonial aspirations, are the first to toss their poisonous spears. As they move in for the kill, each makes vocal noises which unnerves the lion, causing it to attack. When the lion lunges at his assailant, the daring warrior, protects himself beneath his handmade, buffalo-hide shield." Our storyteller continued, "Many times the lion inflicts serious wounds on his tormentor. The other hunters retaliate by tossing their spears, until the lion is dead."

The men agreed that they might have remained single under this harsh rite of passage.

Will suggested to Francois they should check out what the local vultures were doing. "If Ol' Yeller is dead, they will be circling above the carcass." Edmond stated that they can smell a dead animal from over a mile away. Their abode is in the top of tall palm trees gives them a bird's eye view of the happenings in their respective territory. These birds of prey help keep our eco system clean." After checking they didn't see any signs of circling birds. Francois made this insightful comment. "Predators are just part of the cycle of life here in Africa. Death is never wasted. What the lion leaves, the hyena feasts on, and any scraps are cleaned up by jackals, vultures, and ants. And finally, the blistering sun removes any traces of the demise."

When we arrived at the blind it was still daylight. Will crawled up in the hide and made several practice shots at several large sausages that had fallen to the ground beneath the blind. Edmond explained, "Believe it or not, zebra, kudu, and others find these sausages, which are harder than a patrolman's nightstick, a real delicacy." The bullet-shaped fruit was approximately two feet long and weighed about 15 pounds. During the night, when one of those heavy sausages fell off, the sound of it hitting the ground nearly scared me out of my skin. Brian jokingly remarked, "My biggest fear is not that the lions will crawl up in the tree and maul me. NO, it's that one of those lethal sausages will break loose and smash all 210-pounds of me into smithereens."

Will announced, prior to each practice shot, where he was aiming, like a pool player calling the pocket where he intends to sink his ball. Sure enough, his arrow from high up in the tree would hit the target at that exact spot. This impressed all his spectators, especially Zuberi, our youngest tracker.

He asked Francois in Swahili, "Has '*Bwana*' used the bow from his childhood?"

When Francois translated the question, Will, now over the half century mark in age, jokingly retorted, "No, just the last 17 years of my childhood."

While the practicing was in progress, the other jeep drug a hunk of the meat down the river bottom in front of the lion's noses. What better way to advertise the fact that our establishment was once again open for business?

That night multiple big, pawed guests showed up for the grand re-opening. They proved to be very coy indeed because they waited until after dark to consume their food, and stole away before daylight, so as not to be detected. They seemed to have rightly surmised that there is NO free lunch and that the generous meal could have some 'strings attached.'

At breakfast, the insatiable hunters gorged themselves on several eggs and seven plate sized pancakes. Will teasingly ordered his grit-filled pancakes by saying, "Another pancake, John, and hold the sand." Will was really feeling the pressure to get his elephant, because there were just a few days left before we had to pack up and head back to the main camp.

Today was Francois' birthday. Before leaving, I busied myself by tending to some party preparation details. I had brought along items to celebrate Will's success with an elephant. Since that prospect held little promise, I decided to throw our Libra a surprise party. I asked the cook to bake a birthday cake, but John informed me, "Madam, the assistant cook does not have the expertise to make a cake in these remote circumstances." Since necessity is the mother of invention, I told him I would stick the candles in a loaf of his homemade bread. I gave both servers balloons to blow up and place around in the dining area as decorations.

We left camp with high hopes that we could pull off a fun surprise party for our safari leader. Today our jeeps passed by Ol' Yeller's favorite hangouts, but we were unable to find our four-legged friend. In fact, there were very few animals down at the river. Francois thought perhaps our cruising by so often had caused the animals to be uneasy about drinking during daylight hours. I presumed that the animals were probably plain sick and tired of watching us roll by, like teenagers dragging Main Street.

One of the few elephants in sight that day was a cantankerous old one-tusker. According to Edmond, "This one tusked elephant is notorious for being ornery enough to charge vehicles that get in his path." We made sure to steer clear of the 'half-masted' bully. Edmond continued, "It would, in fact, be an error to regard any elephant as passive. The so-called popular belief that only rogue elephants are dangerous is wrong. Those who believe otherwise have become one with the dust without even their just due of gradual disintegration."

We only spotted one other lone bull and during the day Will made three separate stalks on him. Although we spent considerable time and effort on this animal, for one reason or another, a good shot never materialized. Kisenga said that he did not feel quite right about this *tembo*. Will decided that we should heed his sage advice and not pursue the bull any longer.

On our walk out of the bush, I finally achieved my unexpressed, but much hoped for personal goal of keeping pace with our fast-moving white hunter, who was in his usual rush to get back to the blind before dark. I managed to catch up with him and I walked back to the jeep at his side.

We needed an excuse to lure our birthday boy back to the campsite for his party. Will fibbed by saying, "Jeannie's asked to sleep in the blind tonight, so we need to get her things from camp." Fortunately, Francois played right into our hands. Denny acted as our decoy. His job was to keep Francois occupied for as long as possible down on the river bottom behind camp.

Meanwhile, we hustled around getting the finishing touches together for the surprise get together. Everybody dressed up in their party hats and multi-colored leis. I could tell from the worker's reactions that they had never seen anything like this before. I had brought along an assortment of hilarious stick-on moustaches. The men were good sports as they patiently waited their turn to receive the fake hair that we attached to their upper lip. Rama showed up with the bread which became a 'loaf cake' in every sense of the word. While Carlo was at main camp, he was apprised of the surprise affair and grabbed a bottle of champagne. The Italian was busily shaking it up to let his friend have a blast of the bubbly when he arrived on the scene.

Denny could no longer curtail the impatient safari leader. Francois came bursting into the eating area to see what was taking us so long. Luckily, we were ready. We jumped up from our hiding place behind the dining table and yelled, "Surprise!" Carlo aimed the bottle, in his counterpart's direction, as he simultaneously loosened the cork. He released the pressure and a salvo of wet, sticky champagne burst through the air heading toward Francois. I honestly believe that from the look on his drenched but smiling face, that we had put one over on the camp's commander. The air rang with noisemakers mingled with a rousing chorus or two of "Happy Birthday." The Mad Hatter then blew out the candles embedded in the center of his makeshift cake.

Since shopping for gifts was impossible, he unwrapped an unusual assortment of presents. He chuckled as he read aloud the sentiment I had written on the flyleaf of the paperback novel, *South Africa*, by James Mitchener. It read: Happy Birthday to my favorite chief of the 'Wandering Robos.' This unscheduled celebration proved to be a pleasant break from the grind of the safari. I noticed that the tension in Francois' face eased a bit following the merriment. He had put forth great effort, to make sure we were well cared for and having a successful safari. It pleased me to see him relaxing and enjoying himself for a change.

As the men were preparing to leave for the blind, I decided why not join them. Japhet tossed my bedding into the jeep and off we went for my fourth and final night in the 'penthouse suite.'

Once settled in our night nest, I opened the plastic container's lid, which housed the birthday dinner, with great fanfare. This evening's meal was less than an epicurean delight. It was only plain white rice. When I whispered, "Dinner is served in the main dining room of the Treetop Towers," we all dived into our pillows trying to muffle the laughter. Once we had gained our composure, the birthday celebrant opened his serviette, dumped out a huge portion of rice, then started eating with such gusto that one would have suspected he had been served pheasant under glass.

I have vivid memories of the next morning. At first light I heard a noise at the bait. I awakened Francois and Will, and they quietly inched upward for a peek. There standing within range was a youthful male lion and lioness, but not the big lion Will was after. From our 'stick observatory,' we watched in fascinated silence as the pair ate their fill and then went on their merry way.

Chapter 22

A Good Omen

Because this was the next to the last day of the hunt, Francois did not want to waste even a second of our precious time going back to camp. He instructed the cook to bring us a 'curb-service' breakfast of pancakes and fresh pineapple. In addition to our food, Japhet sent along some good news. "I found '*Mama's*' watch buried in the sand beneath her wash basin."

Perhaps this was a good omen that our luck with the elephants was about to change for the better. While freshening up in a puddle of river water, Francois looked up in time to see a lone bull emerging from the brush several hundred yards away. He was packing a pair of worthwhile tusks so Will, Francois, Kisenga, and the film crew begin their stalking.

After an hour or so, the solitary colossus got a whiff of human scent and started searching around for its source. Attempting to avoid detection and possible destruction, the panic-stricken men scurried about like a disturbed colony of ants.

Edmond said, "Bulls aroused by the scent of man often attack at once with unbelievable speed for their size. His trunk and feet are his weapons in the distasteful business of exterminating a mere human. It is not surprising that the bull was on to them, because no animal has a better sense of smell. In fact, they depend more on their olfactory abilities than any of their other senses."

Fortunately, something else got the bull's attention, and he ambled off in another direction. The now liberated men, returned to the jeeps to review their close brush with fate.

As the sun rose higher, in a sky devoid of clouds, our party once again passed by the one tusker who gave every sign of being in his usual testy mood.

About mid-morning the trackers spotted a decent bull with shorter, but stouter ivory. The jeeps jerked to a halt in a shady spot along the edge of the oven-like riverbed. The first team silently slid out for a closer inspection. In the unremitting heat, Lemunduli the skinner, and I took turns watching the stalking activities with the aid of my binoculars. Around noon, we received a thumbs up signal from the hunters, and we eagerly caught up with them to see what it meant. When we arrived, they were all standing around in a circle planning a strategy for stalking the wounded bull.

Will excitedly told me, "For the first time my shot has hit 'pay dirt.' The only thing showing are the feathers!"

This shot is what everyone had been hoping for. It meant Will might be able to cull the largest land animal on earth with his bow! Francois and Edmond had repeatedly stressed that the arrow must make full penetration because of the depth of its vital organs.

After consuming some edibles from my backpack's provisions, we set out to pursue the wounded bull. We trailed, for miles, one behind the other through the bush following his blood trail and smelly droppings. Finally, we had our long-nosed giant under surveillance. Surprisingly, he showed no signs of being wounded. However, he occasionally emitted a low rumbling noise which sounded like distant thunder before an approaching rainstorm.

In defiance of repeated requests not to do so, we inched ever closer to see what was happening. During the afternoon, Will made an additional shot, which missed its intended mark. The bull kept moving as if nothing bothered him except his persistent stalkers.

As the sun was losing its grip in the sky, Francois gave his familiar 'let's go' signal. We beat a path back to the jeeps at a very brisk clip.

As we struggled to keep up with our white hunter, Denny mumbled to me under his panting breath, "Francois only knows two speeds- fast and faster!" I told Denny, "He appears to have steel belted leg muscles like my car tires." The thought of being left in the bush after dark caused me to reach deep into my reserve tank for more energy. To take my mind off my aches and pains I focused on the majestic sunset filling the sky in front of me.

Once safely seated inside the jeep, I could not believe my ears when I heard Francois' insistent voice saying to Will, "I know it's pitch black, but I feel that we should spend the last night of the hunt in the blind."

It has been said that French blood sometimes bestows stubbornness, impervious to good sense, on its bearers. I now knew for a fact of its truthfulness.

It had now been two days since the determined duo had laid their eyes on camp. The two men had become a fighting machine more akin to superheroes than mere mortals.

Once we reached the blind, the jeep's headlights strained to spot the bark covered 'staircase,' which our tired troopers ascended for the tenth and final time.

According to Francois, this would be a world's record for nights spent in the blind! In my estimation these two were the toughest, most determined hunters ever to snicker at the seriousness of a safari.

The rest of us were given orders by Francois, to go pack our belongings and bring them breakfast promptly at 7 a.m. Since tomorrow would be Will's last chance at an elephant, we knew better than to be late.

Chapter 23

Caught in the Blazing Bush

We picked up our 'tree dwellers' on time after having completed preparations for our exodus to main camp. We were three heavily loaded Land Rovers, which contained most of the camp's personnel, bedding, baggage, food, etc. Our unshaven, bedraggled looking menfolk climbed down from the blind with the look and disposition of bears disturbed from hibernation. Although thoroughly worn to a frazzle they were determined to get right at the task of finding their elephant.

As I watched the two men swallowing their last bites of breakfast, I realized how quickly men deteriorate without razor and clean shirt, not unlike a garden that goes to seed unless tended. I had brought both men a change of clothing, shaving gear, soap, and towels, but since time was of the essence, they determined that, accomplishing their goal was more important than their appearances.

We headed straight for the marker Francois had left to aid us in re-locating the tusker's trail. Francois sent one of the vehicles with some of the personnel on ahead to main camp to prepare a hoped for 'homecoming' celebration. How victorious it would be remains to be seen. Francois led the way wearing a pair of tired eyes that looked out through a weary face. Twelve of us spectators followed behind Carlo. Since it was early in the day, the blades of grass were heavily ladened with morning dew, causing the moisture to cling to my pant legs as I hurried by.

We were all hoping to witness the perfect ending to one of the world's epic hunts. Which was assuredly one of the most intense and suspenseful ever attempted!

153

Today would determine whether we would successfully cull the bull or go home empty handed. After walking several miles at top speed, our trackers uncovered the needed evidence; blood stains on the coarse grasses at about the height of a cow's withers. The trackers proceeded with great trepidation through the bush. At length they halted us, and all movement ceased. Kisenga pointed to a chink in the thicket.

Francois firmly grasped Will's arm and guided him towards the bull. Its present, unperturbed pace was characterized by a bold sweeping step. Owing to the spongy formation on his feet, his movement was almost imperceptible except in dead silence. Our bull had not wandered far from where we had left him the previous day. The pungent stench of elephant urine clung in the air.

Will, led by Francois and Kisenga, worked him in close for a shot. Sadly, it missed the heart spot. We all dreaded the consequences of his poorly placed arrow, because now we would have to chase after him for who knows how long. We commenced pursuing the fleeing elephant with the gusto of early morning commuters attempting to catch the last train for work. After an hour or so, the annoyed animal settled back down allowing Will to get off an additional shot. This flawless shot hit the 'bull's eye' and buried itself deep inside its torso. Surely this injury would do him in, but no such luck was to be ours. This big toughie was a long way from being finished.

Carlo led us past the multiple stinging nettle and spiked flora in our path. Will's spectators tried to be quiet and as invisible as possible, but we were not always successful. At this critical juncture, we were told to stay behind at least 100 yards. The fatigued hunter felt his audience was too numerous and overzealous. This was Will's last chance, and he rightfully did not want anything distracting the animal, or his power of concentration.

Francois had determined that the elephant was intentionally leading them on 'a wild goose chase' by leading them deeper and deeper into the hills. About midday, our safari guru decided to put a stop to this nonsense. As Francois said, "We most stop him before we spend the night on 'Mount Kilimanjaro' instead of at the main camp." This was a seemingly ridiculous, but nevertheless true assessment of the situation.

Our white hunter's strategy was simple. Suddenly, the smell of smoke spoiled the pristine air. I could not figure out why he would intentionally set grass fires at a time like this. Carlo explained, "This should help run the bull back toward the river and, in the process, weaken the elephant by keeping him constantly moving. He still appears as 'tough as nails.' In addition, the crackling fires will help hide the noise of his pursuers."

In theory, the fires were great, notwithstanding the problems they caused for us in the 'peanut gallery.' By the time our spectator group got to the place where the fires had been set, the winds had fanned the flames into a serious problem for us. The clear day was now spoiled by the dry grasses being gobbled up by the hungry advancing fire. Clouds of black smoke billowed skyward. The smelly smoke stung my eyes and made breathing difficult. To minimize the noxious fumes, I covered my nose with my neck scarf. The temperature, of the already hot day, rose markedly. The dry grasses and deadwood provided a never-ending source of fuel to the insatiable wildfire.

The blazing bush boomed, hissed, and reverberated as it swiftly moved along its destructive path. Red and orange flames leapt skyward as if trying to compete with the sun. We were in the clutches of a full-fledged bushfire. One in which the wind seemed perversely against us! Panic stricken, we darted about like confused fireflies attempting to skirt the onslaught of flames gobbling up everything in sight.

We were caught between the proverbial 'rock and a hard place'- the raging inferno and the belligerent bull.

Brian had gotten lost from the hunters due to poor visibility caused by flaky ash falling like rain, and the blinding smoke belching forth from the hellish fires. He ran alone in the smoldering bush searching for a friendly face or a way out of this nightmarish situation. Denny and Munduli had also got separated from us. We were unable to concentrate on their whereabouts since our lives were at risk.

By now the deadly fire had gathered enough momentum that the flames where crossing the dry creek bed, causing the combustible flora on the opposite bank to burst into flames.

I was regretting throwing all those enticing life insurance offerings in the trash. It was every man for himself in the blazing bush!

I stumbled along trying to keep up with the men as we darted around the fire. Although I was with veterans of the Selous, they became disorientated in the hectic, smoky confusion and were unsure of our exact location.

In our frantic dashing about, we happened on Brian and his faithful lens. He shouted, "Hey, guys, I'm over here!" I yelled back, "I'm glad you're all right. Where are the others?" Brian answered, "I lost them in the fire. The only thing I've seen is a big eland running for its life. Got any water?" We shared the little we had. Periodically, the men made sure that I got small sips of water even though they went without for my sake. One by one we depleted our water supply until the last precious drops were drained dry. Before long, dehydration exacerbated by strenuous physical exertion and intense heat took its toll on me.

It suddenly dawned on me that we had not seen Denny and Munduli in quite a while. Hopefully, they were safe. My mouth was so dry that I began sucking on dry grasses to generate saliva. The paralyzing heat continued to sap moisture from my weakened body. My head pounded in pain as we pushed onward, ever onward. Just when I thought I could go no farther Denny and Munduli showed up. While lost, they had located some water which they gladly shared. We let the water trickle down our parched throats to help bring us back to life. But no matter how much I drank; I was never satisfied.

Finally, Carlo led us up to the top of a hill which helped us get our bearings. From this vantage point we caught sight of the hunters and the elephant down below. After all the frenzied running from the fire, I had no desire to watch another minute of the seemingly endless chase. All I was interested in doing was staying alive and getting a minute's rest to soothe my throbbing head. Every time there was a lull in the action, I would slump against a tree or rest on the ground.

Edmond came up to me as I was catching my breath and made an astonishing confession. "*Mama*, I need to apologize to you," he blurted out. I asked why. "For years, I've had some misconceptions about white women. I assumed they weren't strong or brave." Then he looked at me and sheepishly said, "What you've successfully persevered on this safari has caused me to change my mind. It is the opinion of everyone concerned, that you truly are a heroine, and I wanted to let you know."

I thanked him and felt honored to have saved the white women of the world from such a misunderstanding. Now all I had to do was live to tell them about it!

Once the fires died out, the temperature moderated and I revived a bit. The men kept asking if I wanted to go back to the jeep. The thought had crossed my mind many times, but I was fully committed to seeing this ordeal through to the bitter end, no matter what. Just your basic elephant chase in the blistering heat would have stymied the most avid safari enthusiast. We had added 'insult to injury' by enduring a potentially deadly bush fire as well. And the day was not over yet!

Bittersweet Finale

The remainder of the day proved quite suspenseful. Will was quickly running out of his specialty arrows, but more importantly, we were out of water again. Things were bad, but wild horses could not have dragged me away from the outcome of this intense struggle. Seven grueling hours had passed since we had left the jeeps. At this stage of the game, accomplishing Will's goal seemed hopeless, but he remained undaunted.

I mentioned to Edmond that the relentless stalk on the elephant seemed cruel. He helped draw me a clearer picture of our situation. "The bull is a goner no matter what. It would be inhumane, as well as dangerous, to leave a seriously wounded animal roaming around in the reserve. Will has to finish him off before sundown with his bow or someone in our party will put him down with a bullet."

The pachyderm was now working his way to the right about forty paces from the men. Francois' years of experience told him, by the way the tusker was behaving that he had been pushed to his limits. The slightest mistake would trigger a full-fledged charge. This unpleasant possibility was still fresh in everyone's mind since that is precisely what Ol' Yeller had done.

Will bravely crept down into a *'mkondo'* for a shot. Much to his chagrin, his razor sharp broadhead got deflected by a bone before meeting its mark. The elephant turned away from Will, giving him the mistaken impression that he would turn and run. Instead, big grey' fooled him. He was obviously searching for the source of his tormentor, and he circled back toward Will. My husband, who was without question a man of considerable courage, stood his ground.

Everyone froze expecting the worst!

My mouth went even drier anticipating what was about to happen. I bit my lip almost in two as I concentrated on my mate's serious predicament. I knew how exhausted Will was and that he probably could not get out of the creek bed before the aggressive bull would be right on top of him. Peering through its tiny eyes, the elephant was unable to get a visual fix on Will's whereabouts. In frustration he turned and moved his mighty frame in the direction of the Njenji River. Relief at that moment took on a new, deeper meaning.

A little while later, Will, with his last ounce of energy, notched and flung his last specialty arrow. The shot was a dud, and the bull simply extracted it from his hide with his nimble nose and dashed it onto the ground in front of himself. The colossus then examined the arrow by gently rolling the shaft over and over with his huge foot. He apparently determined that the arrow had the uselessness of 'teats on a boar,' before tossing it into the weeds. It has been said that 'One man's trash is another man's treasure,' and thus it was, in this instance. Will had Zuberi retrieve the arrow from where the elephant had hurled it. He cleaned it and quickly attached another broadhead.

From this point on, the elephant became visibly weakened and stopped to rest its heavy head on various trees. Francois also noticed that its legs were shaky, indicating that it was becoming increasingly difficult for him to stay on all fours. The bewildered animal also seemed disorientated and indecisive. Many times, the men were sure he could detect their scent, but the dying beast was unable to react to it. Our safari guide knew, now was the time for more aggressive action if his client was going to be the one to put this gray mammoth out of his misery. As Will began bolder maneuvers to push the bull to his limits, it caused us spectators to quicken our pace. While on the go, I kept a watchful eye on the sinking sun's progress, trying to gauge how much more daylight was left.

Suddenly, the ground shook.

Had we just experienced an earthquake?

I heard an unearthly noise and froze with fear.

What was happening??

The men called, "*Mama* come quick!"

As tired as I was, I do not recall expending breath nor muscle to cover the distance to where the others were standing.

I pushed aside some branches to see what they were staring at. In my overtaxed state, it took me a minute to fully comprehend what had happened.

To everybody's surprise, the bull had suddenly crashed to the ground and in the process emitted an unforgettable sound-an eerie death rattle. This pitiful sound rolled hauntingly through his wooded homeland before entering the halls of my heart with full impact.

The elephant went down so unexpectedly that Brian missed filming the poignant scene.

In desperation, the dying bull began frantically rocking back and forth. By mustering all his strength, he managed to raise his heavy frame one last time.

As I witnessed this courageous struggle for survival, emotions of pity welled up inside me, and tears began to flow. I had never witnessed a moment of death, and this distressing experience brought with it an overwhelming sorrow for his plight.

The bull remained upright for only a short while before collapsing in a cloud of dust. This time the camera was rolling. Brian captured the poignant final struggle of this great beast. Will quickly made a perfect heart shot, and the two-day ordeal was finally over.

Ironically, the arrow he had reclaimed from the weeds proved to be the bull's *coup de grace*. Will had taken him down, yes, but was not indifferent to its plight. Our group allowed this aged jungle patriarch the dignity of all free creatures-his moment of respect.

My feelings ran the gamut of joy over Will's success to melancholy over the elephant's demise. My dislike of killing had not changed. To me it was a barbaric practice. This mortally wounded animal brought out my womanly mothering and nurturing instincts. In order to keep from railing at my husband for what he had done, I had to remind myself that we had culled a bull at the bequest of the conservation department. Death is always an emotionally upsetting and heart wrenching process, but in this instance, necessary for the survival of younger animals in the reserve.

Slowly my attitude toward Will mellowed. Exhaustion and lack of nutrition were also affecting my tender emotions. I sank to the earth as tears continued trickling down my dirt-stained face. After a while Will noticed me sitting alone facing away from the congratulatory scene. When my husband noticed me crying, I expected him to show me some compassion. Surely, after three long weeks of faithfully following him through thick and thin, he would give me a hug or a kiss.

NO!

The weary man apparently had nothing left to give. He simply plopped down beside me, put his head between his knees, and for the first time, I saw my mate reduced to tears. Will, like me, seemed genuinely sorrowful to see his valiant foe lying lifeless before us. He said many times during the last two grueling days, he felt confident that the elephant would succumb to the pressure placed on him. After his many disappointments, he thought that perhaps this magnificent creature was perhaps another Ol' Yeller- invincible.

It took a few minutes before we regained control of our emotions. Slowly my attitude toward Will mellowed. Exhaustion and lack of nutrition were also affecting my tender emotions.

Although still upset, I maneuvered my weary body over to get the camera from my backpack. I wanted to take some shots of this momentous occasion. On the way, I crossed paths with Francois who could see I was distraught over the death. His warm French sensitivity could sense what Will could not. He gave me a much-needed embrace. When I told him, "I always cry at funerals," it brought a touch of lightheartedness to the somber occasion.

Francois, who was always thinking ahead, had sent several of his crew to the jeeps. They returned with arms loaded with clanking soda pop bottles and food. I guzzled down the sweet liquid and gradually regained some of my depleted energy. I was too emotional and physically exhausted to eat anything. The men, however, eagerly devoured everything.

We realized that if we did not act quickly, our picture-taking opportunities would soon be gone, as the sun, now a glowing ball of fire, was disappearing behind the trees. They wanted me to stand next to Will in the middle of the group picture. I told them to wait a minute. I spied a nearby puddle of water and washed off what I could of the ashes, soot, and dirt from my face. I added some lipstick and hoped for the best. On this auspicious occasion, Carlo photographed our entire safari party for posterity's sake.

In my estimation, Will's feat should earn him a place in "Ripley's Believe It or Not."

I do not know how he did it, but somehow Francois had managed to maneuver the tusker to within a short distance to our transportation. Our tired, but happy bunch, trudged out of the bush discussing our astounding achievement. Ironically, the only ones to witness our triumphant return were two dirty, green Land Rover jeeps.

Will thought it would be a shame if Brian left Africa without trying out his newly purchased .44 magnum pistol. A nearby target was selected, and he blasted away. Will could see some of the workers were itching to pull the trigger, so they too got off a few shots. Will managed to persuade Kisenga to get in on the action, which made the perfect ending to our final day on safari.

It was completely dark as our jeeps wheeled toward the main camp. The sky overhead was studded with a massive array of twinkling stars. The moon smiled its approval as our vehicles ploughed a path through Sand Rivers for the final time. We soon reached the dirt trail which led inland towards our destination.

During the trip to Kibaoni, we had our first opportunity to review the events of the last two days from our different perspectives. Will mentioned he had tried contacting Denny on his lapel microphone numerous times during the terrible grassfires. He wanted someone to get me to the safety of our jeeps. Denny, of course, had never received those urgent messages because he had gotten lost from our group, and was out of range.

Will, Francois, and I were having such a marvelous time reminiscing that the two-and-a-half-hour trip seemed to go quicker than usual. We only stopped once, and that was to repair a puncture in our right front tire. Since changing a tire was an almost daily occurrence, the men had the procedure down to a fine science and we were on our way in no time 'flat,' to pardon the pun!

During the safari, we all divested ourselves of unwanted inches and weight. Will's 6' 1" frame had slimmed down to 160 pounds. He admitted that he had not been that thin since high school. He was tanned, healthy, and thrilled over the way the hunt had turned out. My husband had paid his hard-earned dues and had come away victorious, thus proving, 'where there's a Will there's a way.'

As we drew closer to the main camp, we could see the glow of electric lights shining off in the distance from the 'metropolis' of Kibaoni.

We were reentering civilization after 19 days in the most remote reaches of the Selous.

The whole camp turned out to greet the victorious hunter and his entourage. Although not a ticker tape parade in New York City, it felt good for others to acknowledge our BIG accomplishment.

The sounds of '*magi ya moto*' rang throughout camp as we rid ourselves of several layers of dirt and smoky soot. Now that we were in a more 'formal' setting, John and Rama were once again decked out in their white serving uniforms. We sat down to a well-deserved feast, complete with ice cubes. We savored, and frankly, deserved every mouthful.

I was curious to know what would happen to the elephant and if any portion of it was edible. Edmond explained "The natives like a portion of the truck and the foot. Years ago, every inch of it was used. The meat was cut into long thin strips, hung on poles, and left to dry in the sun. Sometimes, even the entrails were not left to the vultures and hyenas. The resourceful natives even chopped the bones into chunks and used the nutritious bone marrow to enrich their soups. The hunters also take home many parts for their trophies. Elephant skin makes beautiful purses, belts, billfolds, briefcases, boots, luggage, etc. They are exceptionally durable and last a lifetime."

After dinner Francois, seeking relief from the tension of our lengthy almost nonstop hunt, asked for some muscle relaxants to help him get a decent night's sleep. Everyone teased him and Will that they would probably not know how to act, sleeping in a real 'cot bed.' We offered to lash together a tree stand so they would feel right at home, but for some reason they declined our gracious offer. It was I who did not sleep well.

My body would not shut down and let me relax enough to sleep. On top of the dehydration and over exertion, I was still trying to process the day's traumatic events. I was sad to be leaving the spectacular sights and sounds of the game reserve and being separated from my 'band of brothers.' And last, but not least, I would miss all the daily doses of excitement that this African safari had served up in abundance.

When this safari concluded, I did not want it to be said of me that I did not embrace the chance to do hard things and hopefully emerge victorious. I felt a powerful desire to share my story which would inspire many, especially women.

Chapter 25

Reluctant Farewell

The packing for our return to Dar-es-Salaam began in earnest. Brian informed Will, Edmond, Francois, and me that he intended to interview us to get our concluding perspectives about our successful safari.

Just after breakfast the head cook came into the mess tent to get something out of the refrigerator. While the cook was nearby, I sought Francois' help to get me inside the cook's culinary domain. It was my good fortune that our gourmet chief had a weakness for bow hunters and, luckily, I was his wife. Our safari leader asked John, the serving attendant, to act as my interpreter. I got the red-carpet treatment as he proudly showed me around his meticulously organized, open-air kitchen. The most intriguing feature of his unorthodox, culinary work area was the three unique 'ovens' which were basically just huge piles of ashes and coals: one for pastries, another for bread, a smaller heap where the remainder of the cooking was done.

He indicated that he wanted me to have a copy of his favorite stew recipe, which John read aloud to me as the cook looked on.

ELEPHANT STEW

1 elephant, medium	10 bushels potatoes
2 rabbits (optional)	10 bushels carrots
1 gallon salt	2 bushels onions
1 quart pepper	1 bushel garlic

Cooking Directions: Cut the elephant into bite-size pieces. This should take about a month. Place in the largest pot you can find (or have one specially made). Add water to cover, bring to a boil, and cook over medium-high heat until the elephant is tender (about a week). After it has cooked for 3 days, prepare the vegetables and add them to the meat with salt and pepper. When done, this will serve about 2,000 people. If a few extra people drop in, 2 rabbits could be added to the stew, but only if necessary, as most people do not like to find 'hare' in their stew.

The cook waited for my response to his one-of-a-kind recipe. I let out a BIG laugh!

He could not speak English, but his recipe proved that this masterful out-of-doors cook had a great sense of humor.

I pushed my luck to the hilt and asked John to show me the laundry facility. I was privileged to watch the ironing procedures in process. A man was using a heavy iron full of hot coals. Incidentally, the hot metal relic did a remarkably good press job. For a housewife spoiled with all the modern conveniences, this experience was a fascinating trip back in time.

Before we left camp, Will and I called into our tent several key safari personnel. One by one we thanked them for their superhuman efforts. Each left with a monetary token of our appreciation. We ran out of time, so we gave tips and gifts to Francois for distribution to his personnel.

Brian and Denny used the time to interview Edmond and Francois about their opinions concerning hunting big game with a bow. Basically, they agreed that due to Africa's ever-declining animal population, archery hunting might be a good option. Francois had obviously scrutinized the situation and succinctly summed it up. "Bowmen must spend most of their time either stalking or tracking and doing little killing. With rifles, it is different. You do not need to stalk, and you're doing a lot more killing." Edmond commented, "The conservation department's goal is to preserve the game, while allowing man the opportunity to hunt. The bow seems to be a good way to accomplish both purposes." Everyone, including Will, felt that more research and development was needed to produce more effective broadheads.

At 10:30 a.m. we said goodbye to the 27 camp personnel who had served us so admirably and then hurriedly jumped into the three Land Rovers. It was a four-hour journey to make our rendezvous with our charter flight. Remembering that Chris had left without us on our initial trip, we opted to be early rather than late.

Now that the pressures of the hunt were off his shoulders, Will slept most of the way. Francois and I just sat and visited. Frankly, I was glad to be able to discuss something other than hunting. Our white hunter wholeheartedly agreed that he too had grown weary of the subject that had dominated his thinking day and night for weeks.

At the outset of our adventure, Mrs. Pasanisi had indicated that Francois was from a highly respected French family. I was interested to learn more about his progenitors. He indicated, "My family immigrated to France in the 1300's from Scotland." He proudly said, "One of my great-grandfathers was the general who valiantly led the French Royalist forces to a great victory. For his brave deeds, the King of France did an unusual thing. He knighted all the male members of the general's family. Francois stated, "One can't study French history without reading about my prestigious ancestors."

I felt Francois had inherited and exhibited those same exemplary characteristics during his outstanding leadership of our difficult safari. Having hunted practically around the clock for 18 days, I knew this had been a particularly exhausting experience for him. I was flabbergasted to learn that his next client would be arriving on tomorrow's charter flight. His new client would undoubtedly be full of enthusiasm and energy, and ready to get right at their hunt. It further amazed me that Francois was booked for one hunt, right after another for months, with few if any rest breaks.

This new hunt would probably be 'a piece of cake' compared to our strenuous hunt.

I asked Francois, "If time permits, I would like to stop at some elephant bones I saw on the trip into the main camp. I want to get my picture standing next to one of them." He knew just where to find what I wanted. I hopped out and he stood one of the elephant's leg bones up next to me. It nearly reached my chest. Francois and Carlo took several pictures. Our safari host got the brilliant idea that Carlo should place the bone up on my shoulders for another shot. The weight was overwhelming as the enormous bone began slipping down my back. This predicament made for some hilarious photos with me bowing underneath the weight of the cumbersome object.

At the airstrip, Brian and Denny hurriedly reassembled their equipment for an interview between Francois, Will and me. We enjoyed hearing each other's concluding remarks about the exciting times we had spent together. We also reiterated how grateful we were that our safari had come off so successfully. Many of the events could have stymied the results, but thankfully none had. The delicate camera and sound equipment had functioned perfectly, our health had been good, and no one was seriously injured. We had all gotten along beautifully under adverse circumstances.

History would be the deciding factor as to whether our African venture would be considered as one of the greatest elephant safaris of all time.

We used the remaining time to complete our packing. Luckily, the plane was over an hour late, so we got everything accomplished. Francois promised to come and see us if he ever attended one of the Safari Club International conventions. I found it surprising that he had never been to the United States.

Off in the distance, I detected the low droning sound of our charter plane's engine. It seemed that only yesterday we had arrived to explore this animal paradise. It was then that the thought struck me, as if at a high school graduation, I would probably never see any of these wonderful people again.

The plane drew steadily closer until its ear-splitting noise drowned out all sound except itself. Quite unexpectedly, I felt a lump forming in my throat as I struggled to fight back tears.

We quickly said our thanks to the men who had treated us to a safari *par excellence!* Will paid 'Fearless Faultless Francois' the ultimate compliment by saying, "you are one of the best white hunter in Africa. I have never been in a camp where the guide was as easy to get along with and as knowledgeable as you. In fact, I have not been in any hunting situation where I did not have some little gripe of some sort. I didn't have any here."

Brian also chimed in to praise Francois by saying, "I come from the ranks of anti-hunters. Most of my film making cohorts share the same sentiments. I feel that the culling was warranted because of the large number of game living here. I am not the least bit hesitant to tell anyone that I was a part of this safari."

Unique circumstances had brought us together, and we had formed a strong bond of friendship, love, and respect. We had been through so much together, being constant companions for the past 21 days and nights. It was extremely hard for me to say goodbye. Seasoned soldiers probably feel the same emotions at the end of a particularly tough deployment as they go their separate ways. We had been black and white living and working together in *total peace and harmony.*

I could not help but think that if the politicians would leave well enough alone, the world would be a much better place. There was so little time for us to adjust back into the real world. Oh, how I longed to stay amongst the animals and my friends in this little corner of the world.

Francois must have been having the same feelings of separation anxiety when he turned to me and inquired, "When will I see you again?"

I said, "I have no idea, but I sure hope it's sooner rather than later."

"At Safari Club International in Las Vegas," Will interjected. "Francois, can you arrange your schedule to be there?" I asked.

He winked at me. "I wouldn't miss seeing you again, *Mama*. I had better be there. I may never get you back in the bush again."

"You're right. You may not. I barely lived through this trip." I thought to myself, Chances are, I will probably never see you again, but if not, I'll see you in my dreams!

"But as for you, Will," the white hunter empathetically stated, "We must hunt big game together again with the bow. We must plan our next safari in the forest for the BIG tembo. That is a walking safari, *Mama*. We leave the jeeps behind and carry our camp with us into the deep forests. We'll even carry your bathtub '*Mama*' if you'll join us." We knew his absurd statement was in jest and we all enjoyed one last laugh together.

Francois put his arms around me, and while still laughing, gave me a tender kiss on the neck. It was a moment I shall always cherish. I hugged them all and received a warm goodbye from Manyimancu, whose loyalty to me had been unwavering. When I got to Kisenga he whispered kindly, '*Kwa heri, Mama*,' goodbye."

The pilot revved up the engine, which kicked up clouds of dust. As we lifted off, a hot tear fell on my tanned cheek as I watched the frames of our hunting companions growing smaller and smaller. I hoped Francois would include us in his memories of special clients who had enriched his life while traversing his beloved Africa.

Due to Francois' love of animals, he had spent his life protecting them. I could not fathom him cooped up in an office behind a desk. It would also be a travesty for Kisenga, with his gift for tracking, to do anything else. This untutored black is probably the wisest man on earth in his field. Safaris come and safaris go, but Kisenga just follows the elusive animals and tracks 'em down.

Chapter 25

As we winged our way over the vast expanses of the Selous, I remembered my trip into the reserve. Back then I feared this strange, forbidding place fraught with danger. Now familiarity had removed its mystery. Sand Rivers was now a part of me. I hoped that our bow hunt would be revered and remembered as a special tight-knit group who faced hard tasks, with an 'iron will.'

I doubt that any other women on Earth had seen and done the things that I had been privileged to participate in.

This had been an especially trying struggle to cull a bull elephant, using bow and arrow, in the challenging African bush. Thankfully, we were able to preserve this historical event on film and in my journal for posterity. As we left the reserve, I felt we were leaving behind what civilization should be like, and instead, were heading back into the rat race in our concrete jungles.

We had taken a bull elephant on the last day of the hunt, with the last specialty arrow, as the last bit of daylight lingered in the sky. Who could top that for suspense and adventure?

Departure Difficulties

Our plane headed straight for the airport in Dar, landing right at dusk. Chris taxied over to the private plane's section of the airfield where Dick and his helpers waited to congratulate and assist us with our baggage. Now that the safari was over, I felt sure all the trauma were behind us.

I could NOT have been more mistaken!

Inside the private plane's terminal, we sortied, rearranged, and carefully wrapped the camera gear and film canisters. Denny and Brian would be taking them back to the States that very night. With packing completed, the bed of a small pickup truck and the trunk of a car were loaded to capacity. It was now 8 p.m. and the access gate to the charter portion of the airport was locked. The night security guard came over to inspect our over-loaded vehicles. Our bulging bags looked suspicious, so he escorted our vehicles over to the airport's police station and told us to stay put, while he went inside to converse with his supervisor. No one said much, but our minds were racing.

The situation we found ourselves in smacked of trouble!

Soon several serious-looking black, armed guards headed in our direction. Dick nervously muttered under his breath, "The penalty for filming without permission is three years behind bars." His words tugged at my heartstrings as if a judge had just pronounced the death penalty. Would I ever see my children again?

The officers propped their rifles against the building. Inwardly, we were dying a thousand deaths, as they commenced digging around in our bags, the ones we had just meticulously packed. Dick could not believe that we were experiencing more worrisome problems, and he was not the only one! Despite his diplomatic sweet talk, our safari assistant was unable to dissuade the burley officers from performing their search. They ended up dumping most of the contents out onto the ground. We could do nothing except appear pleasant and helpful, but inwardly our hearts pounded in alarm.

When they came to the film canisters, we held our breath!

There was a good possibility that once they spotted the rolls of film, they might confiscate them or ruin the irreplaceable footage. It was our good fortune that they were only looking for contraband: hides, drugs, ivory, weapons, nothing more. Once their investigation was over, we were free to go. We hurriedly packed our belongings and got out of there before they changed their minds.

We felt it best for Dick to help our camera crew get checked in for their flight before something else cropped up. Will gave them $200 cash in case they encountered unexpected expenses like baggage overcharges. We said our goodbyes and gave Denny and Brian our profound gratitude for a job well done! They scurried off with Dick to catch their 10:30 p.m. flight back to the States.

Meanwhile, we caught a taxi downtown to the Kilimanjaro Hotel to spend the night. We needed to settle our safari finances with Philip, the Pasanisi's nephew, who handled his relative's business affairs while they were back home in France. Because of our unexpected detainment, we were late for our appointment. Luckily, he was used to the many problems and delays associated with East Africa. He was patiently awaiting our arrival in the hotel's lobby accompanied by Paul, Francois' next client. He was a young man, who had come to hunt with his mother, from Mississippi. We remarked what a small world it was, because I had gotten my college degree at the University of Southern Mississippi in Hattiesburg. Philip graciously ushered us into the hotel's café for some cold drinks. Paul and I enjoyed catching up on all the happenings in Mississippi, while Philip and Will settled their financial dealings.

After a while Dick showed up with welcome news. "Your film crew is safely on their way back home." This announcement was music to our ears. I enquired of Dick, "Where's the luggage we left with you three weeks ago?" I thought perhaps he might have already sent them up to our room. I detected a blank look on Dick's face. He finally admitted he did not remember us leaving luggage with him. Philip sensed the need to reassure us concerning Dick's competence by saying, "Dick has never lost a client's belongings. I feel confident he will find them." I sincerely hoped he was right, since all we had to our name were the safari shorts and shirt we had been wearing all day. I might add clothing dirty enough to qualify for a T.V. laundry detergent commercial.

In the meantime, Paul invited Will and I to be his guests for dinner in the hotel's rooftop, open-air restaurant. Philip remarked, "Shorts are taboo in the dining room, but I have no doubt that I can get you admitted because over the years, our safari company has given this hotel a considerable amount of business." Philip paved our way for our entrance, by personally escorting us upstairs. He explained to the maître d' that we were clients of the Pasanisi's and were temporarily without our luggage. We were reluctantly allowed to enter the dining room with the welcome that a couple of mangy dogs would receive in a 5-star establishment. The restaurant overlooked the harbor, which in the stark light of day, revealed a city full of ugly, rundown buildings, but under the benevolent cloak of night, the eyesore was transformed into a glittering fairyland.

After a candlelight dinner and some stimulating conversation with Philip and Paul, we went to our room, showered, and fell exhausted into bed. As tired as I was, I, like Scarlet O'Hara, chose to forget my worries over the lost luggage until tomorrow.

During the night I was awakened out of a sound sleep by a loud banging on our door!

Was it the authorities coming to arrest us for filming in the reserve?

I tried waking Will to have him see who was at the door, but he was unresponsive. I crawled out of bed and groped my way to the door to find out who our insistent intruder was. I cautiously cracked the door ajar while keeping the security chain in place. It was none other than Dick and the bellman with our two missing suitcases. Dick had finally remembered leaving them in the security room at the Bahari Beach Hotel. I thanked him for his diligence, gave them a big tip, then went back to sleep. Dick said he would pick us up in the hotel lobby at 5 a.m. When the alarm went off at 4, I would have paid a thousand dollars for a sledgehammer to silence it.

As promised, Dick arrived in the hotel lobby the next day while we were checking out. His arms were loaded with the Maasai bow, spear, shield, and necklace Will had asked him to purchase. We would enjoy displaying and telling about these authentic African artifacts for years to come.

At the airport, we were at the counter, checking in, when Dick asked Will for $20 so he could pay our departure tax. Unbelievably, Tanzania would not accept their own currency but insisted that U.S. citizens pay in greenbacks. Since Will had given all his cash to our camera crew,

Dick accompanied me to the bank to cash a traveler's check. To comply with Tanzania's exchange control regulations, I had to produce the currency declaration papers we had filled out upon arrival into the country. I fumbled around in my purse, then produced the paperwork which indicated we had declared $200 cash. The bank teller questioned what we had done with the money. She did not believe my truthful explanation about giving the money to friends for their return trip home. She flatly refused to cash my check. In desperation, Dick gave us the money so we could catch our flight.

We proceeded to the security area where, in a small private booth, I experienced an embarrassing 'hat-pin-to-shoe-sole' body search by a rude aggressive female employ. It was my first experience with this extremely uncomfortable, Gestapo-type procedure.

I am a proponent of up close and personal relationships, but this took things too far!

During Will's thorough body search, his security officer spotted his expensive top-of-the-line Swiss Army knife. He was in the process of confiscating it when Dick overheard the argument and quickly interceded. He persuaded the security official to leave the knife in his custody until we returned. The officer reluctantly agreed. We thanked and said goodbye to Dick, then proceeded to the gate where our flight was in the process of boarding.

It was then that we discovered a very disturbing oversight.

We had not been issued boarding passes. Somehow Will talked the ticket taker into letting us board for Nairobi.

I have never been so glad to see a plane's door close!

I hoped that we were finally leaving behind all the troubles we had encountered during our short, hectic sojourn in Dar-es-Salaam. I mentally dubbed this country as the 'Hassle Factor Capital of the World.'

We were thrilled when we discovered that our flight was scheduled to make an intermediary stop at the Mount Kilimanjaro airfield. The majestic mountain was a tourist attraction we had not expected to see. When we landed, the famous landmark was nowhere in sight.

Perhaps they had moved the mountain so they could charge extra for Americans to see it?

Shortly after takeoff our curiosity was rewarded. We flew towards the magnificent 19,340-foot snowcapped peaks of the highest point on the African continent. As we soared overhead, we got a perfect view of the glacier nestled inside the crater of the now extinct volcano. The majestic mountain peaks gleaming in the mid-morning sun were a spectacular sight to behold. To our left, we saw the misty, purple hued plains of the Serengeti. The scenery was a National Geographic photographer's dream. We felt fortunate to have witnessed one of the most spectacular sights on the African continent.

Nairobi Nonsense

Nairobi's airport was teeming with hundreds of travelers attempting to get entry permits. There were no organized lines, just a mass of humanity with one thought in mind, being next at the window. While waiting for 'our turn,' I asked Will if he knew how much the Kenyan government charged for entry fees. Since he was not sure, he waded through the sea of passengers to find the answer. The cost was $8 per person.

As we were out of money, I asked one of the airport personnel where I might cash one of my, now famous, $20 travelers' checks. I was informed that the only place that could handle my request was at a bank on the lower level. A visa official helped me through customs and accompanied me downstairs. I took my place at the end of a lengthy line. While waiting to reach the bank teller, I asked the helpful visa officer, "Do I need U.S. dollars or Kenyan currency to obtain our visas?" He told me shillings.

After filling out the exchange control forms, the bank teller gave me my money and I re-joined my husband. When we finally wormed our way up to the window, the testy official insisted that Americans pay in dollars. I protested, saying that one of their own personnel had advised me to pay in shillings. We were told in no uncertain terms that I had been misinformed. Will suggested that since I was heading back to the bank, I might as well get $100 cash for spending money. The same guard ushered me back down to the bank where the lines had grown longer rather than shorter. The same teller was on duty and when she recognized me, she blurted out, "What are you doing back here?" I politely said that I needed dollars to obtain an entrance visa. Without looking up from her paper shuffling, she insisted I give her back the $20 worth of shillings she had just given me. I explained, "I left the money upstairs with my husband, but don't worry, I'll just cash some additional checks which will give us money for the visas plus some spending money."

The impertinent employee demanded that I return the shillings. Not wanting to cause a scene, I dutifully complied with her ridiculous request. I detected that she was getting a great deal of pleasure out of giving Americans a hard time. I retrieved the shillings from Will and got back in line. In time, I successfully reached her cage.

An apt description of where she belonged.

I handed her back their currency. Now she wanted the receipt she had given me when I had gotten the shillings. An essential detail she had omitted mentioning on my previous trip. Yes, you guessed it, my husband had the needed paperwork. Inwardly, I was seething but tried not to show my frustration at the run around I was receiving. The officer escorting me upstairs for the 'umpteenth' time was very apologetic about the hassle she was putting me through. Feeling like a golden retriever, I got the receipt and retraced my steps along a path I had become all too familiar with. I got back in the queue and finally I completed what should have been an easy transaction.

By now, the crowds at the visa desk were gone except for Will, and two other gentlemen both being of Indian descent. One of the easterners was unable to finish his transactions because he was $3 short of his visa allotment. Will hearing his plight interceded and gave the stranger the needed funds. Bowing deeply, the giant of a man introduced himself as the owner of a restaurant in downtown Nairobi.

His size suggested that perhaps he personally sampled each dish.

The shorter, less stout man was a cook from India. The business proprietor was in the process of helping his new cook immigrate into Kenya. After continually insisting that he wanted to return the favor, our rotund friend asked how long we would be in town. We indicated that we were in transit to South Africa, but our travel plans included a lengthy layover in the city. His unwavering persistence indicated his sincerity, so we reluctantly consented to be his guests for lunch. The restaurateur spoke flawless English, but his cook could only communicate his appreciation with smiles and nods.

While traveling in their car our host and his wife gave us a brief history of their flourishing business. His father had opened the eating establishment 30 years earlier, but now they were partners. Their business, which specialized in East Asian vegetarian cuisine, had blossomed under his tutelage into a popular gathering place for the large Indian population living in and around Nairobi.

We parked in one of the reserved spaces in front of their restaurant. The pungent odor of curry permeated the air as we were welcomed into the restaurant by his father who was appropriately stationed behind the ever-ringing cash register. Since we had no idea what we had committed our taste buds to, we were glad to see a crowd of customers.

Will's rule of thumb is: "A busy eating establishment is usually indicative of great food and excellent service."

My eyes scanned an interesting assortment of customers. I was fascinated by the Indian women robed in beautiful flowing fabrics, some with jewels embedded in their nostrils. Equally interesting were the turban wrapped heads of mysterious looking dark-skinned men in white trousers. Their less traditional clientele were wearing the current fashion rage of the American 'yuppie,' a dark 3-piece business suit.

We were ushered upstairs to a large private dining room which opened nightly for more formal dining. A table towards the back of the now empty room had been set up for our party. As if I had rubbed Aladdin's magic lamp, a jacketed waiter appeared from thin air to pull back my massive carved wooden chair with comfortable red velvet cushions. Once they learned that we were unfamiliar with Indian cuisine, but willing to try it, an unbelievable assortment of epicurean delicacies, fit for a king, were spread before us.

I hasten to add-a king with a huge appetite.

The co-owner and his wife were fasting for religious reasons. It was comforting to learn that they could eat peanuts, and a certain dish made from potatoes, otherwise, we would have felt uncomfortable sampling the savory variety of dishes in front of the hungry couple.

During the conversation, I mentioned the maddening experience I had just been through at the airport. "If travelers have to endure the hassle factors and discourteous treatment I just experienced, they won't have many visitors." Will followed with, "All through Africa, we've had difficulties."

"Yes," said our new friend, "the locals seem to have a chip on their shoulders ever since they took over the government. Their newfound power has gone to their head. When Colonialism became a thing of the past, Black-white relations became very strained." I asked, "So their surly attitudes are not just leveled towards Americans?"

He said, "No, but Americans seem to get the brunt of it. Sometimes they just lump all nationalities together and show hostility towards everyone. This is just a stage in their development, like teenagers impressed with their newfound freedom. For sure, they can be ornery, however, try not to be offended and take it personally. "

Our plane left at 3 p.m., so our hosts felt it advisable to have us back at the airport an hour prior to flight time. Although we were busy chatting as we traveled to the airport, I noticed that Nairobi appeared considerably more modern and prosperous than Tanzania. Africa was certainly a continent of contrasts. As we were being dropped off we expressed appreciation for their magnanimous hospitality, which more than over-shadowed our measly $3 gesture.

While waiting in the departure area, one of the airline employees posted the unwelcome news, that our Olympus Airline flight to Johannesburg was delayed one hour. We sat down and settled in for another 'hurry up and wait' situation. There were only seven other passengers waiting to board our flight. One of our fellow passengers, a Frenchman residing in Nairobi, astounded us with the disturbing news concerning our destination. He said, "It's unbelievable that South African aircraft can no longer land on American soil." This dramatic turn of events was quite frankly astounding. We were aware that South Africa was getting increased pressure concerning their government's racial segregation policies. While on safari, the apartheid issue had blossomed into worldwide proportions. He indicated that the U.S. government, South Africa's longtime ally, had joined the ever-growing number of countries that were applying crippling, political and financial sanctions on them.

Once we went through numerous security checks and a body search required for departing Kenya, we found ourselves upstairs in the departure lounge. Our astute French acquaintance brought to our attention the numerous technicians hovering around one of the 747's engines. The massive jet engines made the mechanics appear almost dwarf-like. Difficulties with one of the plane's engines, kept us on the ground several more hours before we could board the Greek airliner for a 4-hour flight to the southern tip of Africa.

Will had become somewhat of a 'zombie,' since the pressures of the hunt were over, by napping every chance he got. This gave me the opportunity to mentally revisit our trip. What a thrill our time in Africa had been.

In a way, adversity had been my passport to self-discovery.

I had managed to tolerate and deal with Third-World ineptness. On the long stalks, I had kept up with the men and had coped with daily doses of danger. I had been accepted and even admired by the hunters and natives. I had taken copious notes which would be indispensable when piecing together the upcoming documentary. I felt good about having been an integral part of one of the world's most thrilling and demanding adventures.

It suddenly dawned on me that what I had lived through should be more than a bunch of cold accurate notes. I should capture this whole glorious affair in a BOOK! This would give others the opportunity to enjoy our exciting one-of-a-kind adventures.

Will woke up wondering what was happening. We entertained the possibility that this flight might be practically empty judging from the small number of passengers awaiting to board in Nairobi. We envisioned our weary bodies stretching comfortably across several unoccupied seats. As we boarded, dreams of all our creature comforts crumbled like crackers into a steaming bowl of soup. We were lucky to have two seats together. The plane was packed with Europeans traveling in our direction. Many of the passengers complained that they had not been allowed to disembark during the lengthy engine repairs. Instead, they had been held captive for hours in the hot, crowded airplane. So, those of us who had been waiting in the comfortable air-conditioned terminal, did not have it so bad after all.

Chapter 28

Exploring South Africa

Upon landing in Johannesburg, hundreds of travel-weary passengers eagerly escaped their confinement and flooded into the arrival hall of the Jan Smuts Airport. Lengthy lines now formed across the freshly polished marble floors in front of their respective custom's booths. We were advised, by those familiar with the eccentricities of African political hassles, that we should not have our passports stamped in South Africa. If we did, we would never be allowed to re-enter Kenya and Tanzania to pick up the safari gear that we had left with Dick.

When it was our turn at passport control, Will mentioned that we anticipated having a lovely holiday in South Africa, but visiting here might cause us difficulties considering our travel arrangements. The intuitive customs agent read our itinerary, perceived the problem, and without uttering a word pounded an official government seal on a separate piece of paper, instead of in our passports. It was a pleasure to, once again, be amongst people that had 'no axe to grind' with Americans.

Due to worldwide political pressures their currency, the Rand, was horribly devalued. Consequently, the exchange rate was extremely favorable to our dollar. The cost of many goods and services was about half the price we would ordinarily pay. For instance, our very ample accommodations in the American based hotel chain, adjacent to the airport, cost a mere $25 a day, which included a delicious all-you-can-eat breakfast buffet. We were able to direct dial our family. It was wonderful to hear their voices and learn that everyone was doing fine. We shared a few juicy tidbits concerning our successful safari before concluding the expensive conversation.

After the first good night's sleep I had experienced in a month, Will decided we should explore the country. This sounded like a good

185

idea until I found out that they drive British style, or to Americans, on the wrong side of the road! I was glad it was Sunday, a low traffic day, when we rented a car, because driving in the left lane felt unnatural and was downright frightening.

At the rental car agency, I joked with Will, "We should rent a James Bond style car with a passenger ejection seat, in case you mistakenly get on the wrong side of the road." The fun-loving agent teased us by saying, "Sorry to disappoint you, but rentals of that description have been reserved by other American tourists." It was a nice change of pace to find someone helpful that had a good sense of humor. We asked directions to the nearest Church of Jesus Christ of Latter-Day Saints. In her directions, the lady mentioned, "The closest chapel is in Kempton Park, only a few kilometers from here. Just turn right at the second 'robot'." I turned to Will to see if he understood what she meant. He was unfamiliar with this terminology too. The agent laughed and explained that 'robot' was their country's slang term for traffic signal or stoplight.

The South African population was an interesting mix of people, thus the need for two official languages. The smattering of Swahili we had learned was of no use to us here. Since we did not speak any Afrikaans, it was comforting to find that almost everyone was bilingual, speaking both English and Afrikaans. Thankfully, most of the signs were in both languages. Afrikaans is a hodge-podge of many languages developed primarily from Dutch. Schoolchildren are also taught the native language of their province. Students in Natal province learn to speak Zulu; those in the northern Transvaal provinces, learn Sotho, etc.

South African English resembles the standard King's English, with Afrikaans terminology sprinkled in. The white population numbered around five million. About three-fifths are Afrikaners, or 'Boers' as they are sometimes referred to. Their ancestors settled the country in the 1600 and 1700s, from the Netherlands, Germany, and France. Today's Afrikaners make up most of the white population in rural areas and are highly concentrated in larger cities like Johannesburg and Pretoria. The remaining whites, hail from England, Ireland, and Scotland. They settled in the southernmost regions of the Cape and Natal provinces. The remainder of the country's population is either Black or colored (a mixture of white and black). The Black people are by far the most numerous at over 25 million (about half of them are colored).

After church, we headed to the capital city of Pretoria. It was a 45-minute drive on the freeway, northeast of the sprawling metropolis of Johannesburg. The country became the gold capital of the world when huge gold deposits were discovered in the 1800s. We saw numerous huge piles of mine tailings on our way out of town. The road system was modern and well-maintained. We were impressed as we passed underneath the largest concentration of power lines that we had ever seen. This was no lesser developed country. The crops in the fields appeared lush and the farms lucrative. Most of their automobiles were new and well maintained.

Pretoria was a beautiful capital city where about 50% of the office space housed government agencies. These large buildings were nestled beneath gorgeous jacarandas trees, full of purple flowers, lining many of the streets.

We checked into a hotel conveniently located near the city center. Although the dark skins outnumbered the whites, ten thousand to one, I felt amazingly comfortable walking all alone exploring the city. The stores, shopping arcades, and malls I visited sold good quality merchandise and their supermarkets stocked an abundance of delicious foods. Due to the many similarities and the fact that everyone we encountered spoke English, it was not a place that engendered culture shock. I enjoyed selecting from a wide variety of unique African handmade gifts for family and friends.

On October 15, we were scheduled to catch a late afternoon flight to Nairobi, but the anti-theft locking device installed in the rental car's windshield malfunctioned. For some reason, when Will tried to open the car it simply would not allow him entry. Consequently, we were unable to return the car to the drop-off location at the Johannesburg airport. We frantically hailed a cab in front of our hotel in Pretoria. The taxi driver could not believe his good fortune when we said our destination was the Jan Smuts airport in Jo'burg. It was a long trip that would earn him unexpected income.

We were cruising down the freeway, and Will was taking a snooze, which he jokingly referred to as, "Closing my eyes to check for light leaks." Suddenly the car's power went haywire, and our speed got progressively slower and slower. By the time we arrived at the terminal the taxi did not have enough 'juice' left to climb up the departure ramp. Will paid the driver, grabbed our bags, and we ran to catch the plane.

We made our flight but talk about a close call.

Time in South Africa had provided us with the much-needed respite from the intensity of the grueling safari. We experienced perfect weather, delicious food, friendly people, and low prices.

Chapter 29

Backtracking to Tanzania

It was almost midnight when we landed in Nairobi. Our travel plans included an overnight stay at a hotel in the downtown area. The next morning during a hearty brunch, Will was in a jovial mood and said, "We've gone through a lot together, haven't we?" Then with a big smile across his tan face said, "Remember the time we were moose hunting in Alaska?"

"How could I ever forget that dirty trick you played on me," I said. "As you were taking off from the slew where we were camped, you spotted a big moose, and like a wild man, whipped the plane around into a sharp bank. Then slammed your 'Super Duck' (his twin-engine amphibious Widgeon airplane) down on the water."

Will teased, "When I opened the door and bailed out onto the wing to get a shot, I'd love to have had an 8 X 10 of your facial expression."

"Yeah, you know very well I'd never piloted a plane. I had no clue what to do. I found out the hard way, it was nothing like driving a car."

While swallowing some guava juice, I remembered the last time I had seen his 'Super Duck.' We experienced twin engine icing on the way from our home in Las Vegas to Salt Lake City, which caused us to go down like a rock in the Utah desert in the vicinity of Delta.

"The las time I saw it the snow was falling on your wrecked plane lying there wheels up, all crushed and dirty. I'll bet you miss that old bird, don't you?"

189

"That airplane and I had lots of fun times together," he said while thinking back on the plane crash our family had miraculously walked away from, in October of '79. I could tell that this was a painful memory, so I quickly changed the subject to the time we had hunted elk.

"It's a tossup," I continued while buttering a roll. "What's a tossup?" he said attempting to switch mental gears.

"Well, it's difficult to say which is my favorite wild animal sound. I can still recall the echo-like sounds of the elk bugling outside our tent, on our horseback camping trip into the mountains of Montana. However, I must admit there is nothing that remotely rivals a lion's roar in the bush. There is no way anyone can aptly describe either of those sounds without hearing them in the wild. I'm glad I joined you on both adventuresome outings." Will pulled off his glasses and peered at me through his steel blue eyes. "You know, you're definitely pioneer stock, Jean. I'm glad you came along."

Nairobi still retained its reputation as being a frontier town that was the last outpost of civilization in Africa for some 2,000 miles. Its narrow streets were jammed day and night with noisy vehicles driven by impatient drivers honking their horns. Add to this, thousands of natives and East Asian Indians bustling about, and you have the typical street scene in Nairobi.

I exchanged money at the hotel so I could complete my shopping. In the area near our hotel, prices were sky high. I was determined to find a marketplace where I could buy reasonably priced souvenirs.

Once outside the hotel, my white skin was in the minority. I was like a scoop of vanilla ice cream melting into a hot fudge sauce. I visually searched for and found a well-dressed, English-speaking gentleman who indicated that he knew of a nearby market that sold African souvenirs. He indicated that he was heading in that general direction and wanted me to follow him. I disappeared into the honeycomb of this fascinating city and hoped he was not leading me down some 'primrose path.' After we had traveled several blocks he stopped and pointed me towards a building down a side street. I thanked him for his assistance and headed towards the old building.

This place housed a floor to ceiling motherload of African trinkets. Most of the shop owners hailed from India and Pakistan and lived up to their reputation as being shrewd businessmen. Once pegged as an American tourist, the shop attendants, and beggars, approached me. They soon learned that I was no push over, but firm in my resolve not to pay their inflated tourist prices. After some good-natured haggling, an amount was settled upon that we both could agree on.

What they did not realize was that while living in Costa Rica, I had become adept at dickering for the best prices with the local 'Tico' merchants.

I depleted the remainder of my money and with arms loaded, headed back the ten or so blocks to my hotel. On the way, it dawned on me that I was not far from the famous Ngong Hills located near Nairobi. These hills were made famous by author Karen Blixen in her book entitled *Out of Africa*. This famous memoir documented her time living in British East Africa (now Kenya). Karen owned and operated a coffee farm at the foot of these hills. She was portrayed in the movie, of the same name, by actress Meryl Streep. Karen's story became a film that won 7 Academy awards. As the winner of best picture, it immortalized her love for Africa and Denys Finch Hatton, portrayed by Robert Redford. Denys, a big game safari leader, died in 1931 in a tragic accident, when his plane crashed and burned. His tombstone is located only 5 miles west of the nearby Nairobi National Park.

After her coffee farm burned, a grieving Karen moved back to her native country of Denmark. She later received a letter from an African friend saying, "The Maasai have reported to the district commissioner at Ngong, that many times, at sunrise and sunset, they have seen a lion and lioness on Finch Hatton's grave. The pair, which reminds me of you and Denys, have stood and lain on the grave for a long time."

This message really touched my soul.

Back at the hotel, I loaded my suitcase with my latest acquisitions, we checked out and took a taxi to catch the 3:30 p.m. flight back to Dar. Upon landing, we spotted our reliable safari assistant Dick. Because of his connections, we short-circuited some of the red tape at customs. He had booked us for a half-day stay at the Kilimanjaro Hotel. Once inside the room, Will got busy sorting through the bags filled with our well-used hunting paraphernalia. Will felt sure we would return to hunt with Francois and carting all those bulky items back and forth, across the world, was expensive. I made a list of the things to be left with Dick, while Will enquired about his Swiss Army knife. Dick indicated, "I put it inside your luggage." Will never found it. Admittedly, it was an irresistible item in such a poor country.

Dick and his wife were our guests for dinner that evening at the hotel's roof-top restaurant. Dick's wife was very affable, but due to the language barrier, it was difficult to communicate. Following the meal, we dashed off to the airport for our evening departure back to the States. We said our goodbyes hoping to book another safari in the future.

Chapter 30

Homeward Bound

Our plane thrust us skyward, heading for the European continent. After the meal service, I felt drowsy, as if drugged by a sleeping potion. Next thing I knew, it was morning, and we were landing in Holland. It was a lovely sunny morning exactly right for exploring this scenic capital city. Since we had a five-hour layover, we quickly stashed our carry-on luggage in an airport locker and walked over to the train station, which was conveniently located adjacent to the airport's terminal building.

We purchased round-trip tickets into Amsterdam's city center. Our train sped past their beautifully manicured countryside. Everything appeared so fresh and green compared to the parched conditions we had experienced on the safari. The landscape was dotted with the essential navigable canals and locks, but not a single windmill came into view.

Once inside this charming city, we ambled down cobblestone streets still damp with heavy morning dew and paused on a bridge to enjoy a melody cranked out by a large antique barrel organ. Underneath, glass-topped boats glided past, packed with curious tourists craning their necks to get a glimpse at the tall historic buildings.

The day was young and the chill in the air prompted us to stop at a sidewalk cafe to enjoy a steaming cup of Holland's famous hot chocolate. Once warmed, we walked past an area where vendors were busily setting out a large assortment of beautiful fresh flowers. The perfumed aroma permeating the air was sure to get the attention of the locals passing by.

In our wanderings through the picturesque city, we found ourselves in the infamous, police-protected prostitute district. Each evening, ladies of dubious reputation strut around their houses of ill repute, decked out in outlandish costumes, hoping to lure in some patrons. I suppose you could say, on safari we did pretty much the same thing by baiting the lions and the leopard.

There was even an occasional large glass viewing case erected right next to the sidewalk. One was complete with an oversized gaudy, gold chair and gilded mirror. These glass showcases were used as 'come-ons' by some of the more enterprising women. It was much too early in the day for most of the hookers to be outside, but we did spot a few scantily clad diehards sunning their shapely bodies.

On the way back to the station, we bought a pair of wooden clogs and a traditional Dutch dress and lace cap for our daughter, who would turn three in a few days. Before we knew it, the time had slipped away, and we were once again passengers on the train heading for the airport.

Once I got back home, I knew my opportunities to write would be few and far between, because of family, church service, and school matters which would rightly take priority. On the trip to Chicago, I played catch-up, writing in my journal. I wanted to capture my feelings concerning our unprecedented adventure while it was still fresh in my mind.

My initial clouds of doubt and fears concerning the safari dissipated when I began experiencing Africa's mesmerizing allure. Although I encountered many difficult dangerous experiences, I felt fortunate to have seen and done what others only dream of. The reserve helped me gain a perspective on the need to protect and professionally manage Tanzania's wildlife. Their extraordinary creatures draw visitors from all over the world and are a veritable goldmine of revenue for such a poor country.

One cannot deny that these animals existence is extremely fragile due to an increasing human population, coupled with unscrupulous hunting practices. Civilization will be the loser if these unique animals only exist as curiosities in zoos. Big lumbering elephants would never have the pleasure of knocking down trees, drinking at the river's edge, and spraying river water onto themselves. Caring females would not be around to teach and protect their young. Witnessing Africa in its raw natural state has provided me with precious memories and a desire to share my 'walk on the wild side' with others.

Granted, Will's initial odds of getting an elephant ranged from not good to zero. However, he accomplished his lofty goal by following a few simple steps: intense desire, continuous preparation, seeking professional help, and diligently pursuing his goal. By consistently doing these things, this middle-aged man had 'beaten the odds' and succeeded in taking a bull elephant with his bow!

A feat only accomplished by 3 or 4 others!

Once we landed at Chicago's O'Hare International Airport, we stretched our legs inside the large terminal building. It was not long before a vendor had successfully lured me into their business with the tantalizing smell of popcorn.

Now I knew how the hungry lions felt.

While killing time, we passed an ice cream parlor. The next thing I knew, we were feasting on some exotic flavor encased in a crunchy waffle cone. Normally, I am not even fond of the gooey, cold stuff, but the closest thing to a sweet we had eaten in over a month was the jam on our toast, and our resistance levels were at an all-time low.

We then boarded the plane for the last leg of our journey. As the plane taxied to a stop in Salt Lake City, it felt great to once again be on familiar territory. During our absence, the multi-colored leaves had lost their grip on the trees. The air felt especially frigid since we had just come from the tropical temperatures of Africa. The icy wind felt bone chilling as we loaded our bags into the truck.

It had been two days since we had gotten a good night's sleep, so we opted to stay overnight in a hotel before tackling the four-and-a-half-hour drive home, in the dark, on icy roads. As we followed the familiar path to Idaho, on October 18, I felt a closeness between my husband and me after having shared this remarkable journey. In the past, when he had returned from his South African safari, he brought back stories and trophies of his trip, but I simply could not relate to his experiences and struggles. Now I could better understand what he had gone through.

We began honking the horn as we pulled into our driveway. The kids heard us and ran outside to greet and hug us. We had a glorious reunion with our excited children. They were glad to see us and to get their African souvenirs. In my estimation, Shauna and Cassie, our family helpers, were the real unsung heroines who survived tending the children. Undoubtedly, these ladies were the happiest of all to see us return.

After a month's absence from the normal cares of our busy lives we settled back into our daily routines and watched our suntans fade as the winter months drug on. Remembrances of my extraordinary journey hang in the halls of my mind like treasured trophies. These recollections will remain vividly alive until I can return to the Africa I love.

Some months later, the frustrations of Africa followed us back home. As expected, Will's elephant tusks were delivered to his taxidermist. However, believe it or not, the elephant's head was missing its ears, and due to improper handling, the hide was rotten and unusable. So, in the end, Ol' Yeller and his big-eared, long-nose cohorts had gotten the best of us and are laughing about how they all managed to ELUDE us in one way or the other!